CRIB
NOTES

A RANDOM REFERENCE
FOR THE MODERN PARENT

Amy Maniatis

and

Elizabeth Weil

QUADRILLE

*Every effort has been made to trace the ownership of all copyrighted material in-
cluded in this volume. Any errors that may have occurred are inadvertent and will
be corrected in subsequent editions, provided notification is sent to the publisher.*
Barbie is a trademark of Mattel, Inc. Copyright © 2004 by Mattel, Inc. All
rights reserved. Pp. 24, 25, and 84 from *The Third Chimpanzee* by C. Jared
Diamond. Copyright © 1992 by C. Jared Diamond. Reprinted by permission
of Random House. P. 61 from *The World of the Newborn* by Daphne Maurer
and Charles Maurer, copyright © 1988. Used by permission of Daphne
Maurer and Charles Maurer. P. 105 from *Wong's Essentials of Pediatric
Nursing*, sixth edition, by D.L. Wong, M. Hockenberry-Eaton, D. Wilson, M.
L. Winkelstein, and P. Schwartz. Copyright © 2001 by Mosby, Inc. Reprinted
by permission. P. 127 from *Babyhood* by Penelope Leach. Copyright © 1974,
1976 by Penelope Leach. Used by permission of Dorling Kindersley. P. 142
from 'Infants' Perception of Natural and Distorted Arrangements of a
Schematic Face' by D. Maurer and M. Barrera, in *Child Development* 52: 197.
1981. Reprinted by permission of the Society for Research in Child
Development.

First published in English by
Chronicle Books LLC, San Francisco, California.

This edition first published in 2005 by
Quadrille Publishing Limited, Alhambra House,
27–31 Charing Cross Road, London WC2H 0LS

The rights of Amy Maniatis and Elizabeth Weil have been
asserted by the Copyright, Design and Patents Act 1988.

Cataloguing in Publication Data: a catalogue record for this book is
available from the British Library.

ISBN 1 84400 218 7
Printed and bound in China

for

Lucy,

Chloe

and

Hannah

CONTENTS

CONTENTS *continued*

CONTENTS *continued*

CONTENTS *continued*

INTRODUCTION

If you've been pregnant for more than five minutes, you've probably noticed that almost every book on pregnancy and parenting talks to you like, well, somebody's mum. That's why we wrote *Crib Notes* – an intentionally selective, incomplete and largely impractical series of lists, charts, diagrams and facts pertaining to the modern breeder. It contains little that is strictly necessary for the raising of a child, but almost everything you really want to know. We've taken the high brow, the low brow, the fun, the esoteric, the stimulating, the informative, the economic, the hilarious, the philosophical, the entertaining, the practical and the historical, and boiled it all down to the nuggets. We know *Crib Notes* won't replace the old references, but we hope you'll enjoy reading it as much as we enjoyed putting it together.

HOW TO TELL IF YOUR CHILD
IS THE DALAI LAMA

Large ears

Long eyes

Eyebrows curving up at the ends

Streaks on the legs

A mark in the shape of a conch shell
on the palm of one hand

The ability to distinguish articles
belonging to the previous Dalai Lama
(such as spectacles,
a silver pencil,
an eating bowl,
a black rosary,
a yellow rosary,
a walking stick
and a small ivory hand drum
used in religious devotions)

PERCENTAGE OF CHILDREN BORN
BY DAY OF THE WEEK

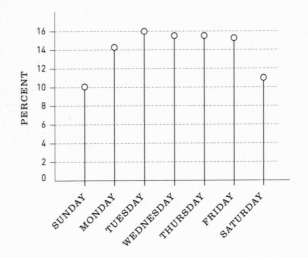

WHAT'S A SECOND COUSIN TWICE REMOVED?

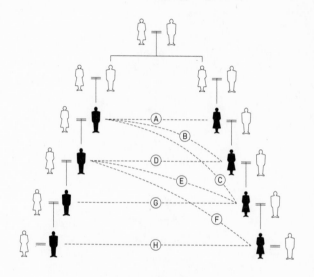

Ⓐ First Cousins

Ⓑ First Cousins, once removed

Ⓒ First Cousins, twice removed

Ⓓ Second Cousins

Ⓔ Second Cousins, once removed

Ⓕ Second Cousins, twice removed

Ⓖ Third Cousins

Ⓗ Fourth Cousins

WHAT KIDS WANT TO BE WHEN THEY GROW UP, ACCORDING TO THE JUNIOR ACHIEVEMENT ENTERPRISE POLL

Business person

Doctor

Teacher

Lawyer

Entertainer

Athlete

Computer Programmer

Law Enforcement Officer

Fashion Designer

Trade person

Scientist

Journalist

Nurse

Accountant

Engineer

Social Worker

Marketing Specialist

Soldier

Psychologist

Veterinarian

Architect

Cosmetologist

Chef

Physical Therapist

Photographer

OLD WIVES' TALES FOR PREDICTING
THE SEX OF AN UNBORN BABY

	MALE	FEMALE
Belly, shape	beach ball	watermelon
Belly, position	low	high
Body hair	more	same
Cravings	pickles, meat, cheese	orange juice, sweets
Father	gains weight with mother	stays the same
Foetal heart rate	<139	>140
Morning sickness	mild	severe
Mother displays hands	palms down	palms up
Mother picks up a key	by the round end	by the long end
Mother's dreams	filled with girls	filled with boys
Mother's feet	colder	same temperature
Mother's left breast	smaller than right	larger than right
Mother's skin	smooth	pimply, less attractive
Mother's sleeping position	left side	right side
Pendant swings over mother's palms	back and forth	in circle
Preschool boys	ignore mother	show interest
Sexual aggressor during conception	mother	father

HOW TO MAKE A DOG BALLOON

STEP 1: Inflate a '260' balloon, leaving about 15 centimetres at the end.

STEP 2: Starting at the end you tied, twist off a length of balloon about three fingers long. Hold both sides of the balloon around the twist so it doesn't come undone. This twist is the nose.

STEP 3: While holding the first twist, make two more, holding them all with one hand. These twists are the ears.

STEP 4: Fold the second and third bubbles together, and twist together joints A and B.

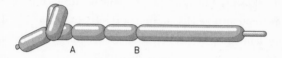

STEP 5: Make another bubble about the length of three fingers for the neck. Then make two more bubbles about twice that size for the legs.

STEP 6: Twist the two leg bubbles together at joints A and B.

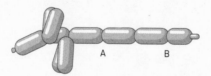

STEP 7: Make a long bubble for the dog's body, and then two more bubbles for the back legs, leaving some length for a tail.

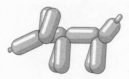

STEP 8: Twist the back leg joints together.

THE RIGHTS OF THE CHILD

The following fundamental principle is extracted from the
preamble to The Declaration of the Rights of the Child,
proclaimed by the United Nations General Assembly on
20 November 1959.

'Whereas mankind owes to the child the best it has to give.'

FORMULAE FOR
COMPOUND INTEREST

P is the principal
(the initial amount you borrow or deposit).

r is the annual rate of interest
(percentage).

n is the number of years the amount
is deposited or borrowed for.

A is the amount of money
accumulated after **n** years, including interest.

If interest is compounded annually:
$$A = P (1 + r)n$$

If interest is compounded quarterly:
$$A = P (1 + r /4)4n$$

If interest is compounded monthly:
$$A = P (1 + r /12)12n$$

If interest is compounded daily:
$$A = P (1 + r /365)365n$$

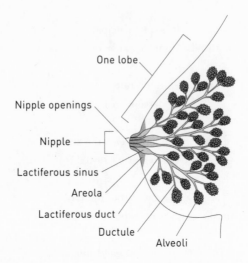

One lobe

Nipple openings

Nipple

Lactiferous sinus

Areola

Lactiferous duct

Ductule

Alveoli

The creation of milk begins in the *alveoli,* which are surrounded by one-cell deep connective tissue known as the *myoepithelial cells.* These cells act like miniature muscles, squeezing the milk into *ductules.* The ductules then converge into the larger *lactiferous ducts.* The lactiferous ducts become wider near their connection to the *nipple,* where they act as collecting and pooling areas for foremilk known as the *lactiferous sinuses.* These sinuses are located directly underneath the *areola* and extend into the nipple. Each cluster of alveoli, ductules, lactiferous ducts and lactiferous sinuses is called a *lobe.* There are 15 to 20 lobes in each breast and 15 to 20 corresponding ducts within each nipple. These converge into 5 to 10 ducts, and milk is expelled through 5 to 10 openings in the nipple.

THE MANY CAREERS OF BARBIE

Actress

Aerobics Instructor

Air Force Squadron Leader

American Airlines Flight Attendant

Army Medic

Army Officer

Art Teacher

Artist

Astronaut

Ballerina

Baseball Player

Boutique Owner

Business Executive

Candy Striper (hospital volunteer)

Chef

Concert Pianist

Dentist

Doctor

Downhill Skier

Dress Designer

Engineer

Executive

Fashion Editor

Fashion Model

Figure Skater

Firefighter

Formula 1 Driver

Gymnast

Ice Capades Star

Junior Designer

Lifeguard

Major League Baseball Player

Marine Corps Sergeant

Miss America

Music Video Star

NASCAR Driver

Naval Petty Officer

NBA Player

Olympic Athlete

Olympic Gymnast

Olympic Ice Skater

Olympic Swimmer

Palaeontologist

Pan Am Flight Attendant

Paediatrician

Pilot

Police Officer

Presidential Candidate

Radio City Music Hall Rockette

Rap Musician

Registered Nurse

Rock Star

Scuba Diver

Sign Language Teacher

Singer

Summit Diplomat

Surgeon

Teacher

Teenage Fashion Model

Tennis Pro

TV News Reporter

U.S. Air Force Pilot

UNICEF Ambassador

United Airlines Flight Attendant

Veterinarian

Women's World Cup Soccer Player

WNBA Basketball Player

FEMALES,
AS MALES SEE THEM

The main circles represent female body size relative to male body size of the same species. The smaller circles represent relative size of breasts.

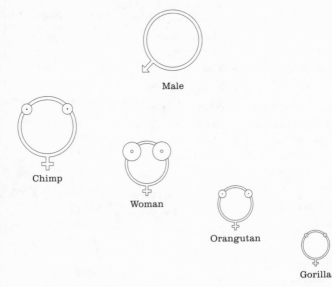

Male

Chimp

Woman

Orangutan

Gorilla

MALES,
AS FEMALES SEE THEM

The main circles represent male body size relative to female body size of the same species. The arrows are proportional to the length of the erect penis. The twin circles represent testis weight relative to that of penis.

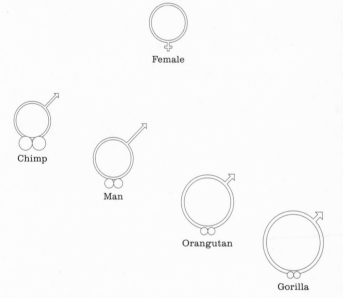

Female

Chimp

Man

Orangutan

Gorilla

MEAN DURATION OF COITUS
IN VARIOUS SPECIES

Mosquito	3 seconds
Common Chimpanzee	7 seconds
Pygmy Chimpanzee	15 seconds
Whale	30 seconds
Elephant	30 seconds
Gorilla	1 minute
Duck	2 minutes
Beaver	3 minutes
Human	4 minutes
Orangutan	15 minutes
Marsupial Mouse	12 hours

INSTRUCTIONS FOR
'THE ITSY BITSY SPIDER'

The itsy bitsy spider climbed up the waterspout.

> Touch right index finger to left thumb, and left index finger to right thumb; pivot on upper pair of fingers, continue motion, moving hands towards head.

Down came the rain

> Wiggle fingers down from head to waist.

And washed the spider out.

> Extend arms and hands out from waist.

Out came the sun and dried up all the rain,

> Raise hands above the head, clasp fingers to form a circle.

And the itsy bitsy spider climbed up the spout again.

> Repeat the first movement.

AVERAGE NUMBER OF SPERM
PER EJACULATION
IN VARIOUS ANIMALS

ANIMAL	SPERM (IN MILLIONS)
Mouse	50
Rat	58
Guinea Pig	80
Rabbit	280
Human	280
Sheep	1,000
Cow	3,000
Horse	6,000
Pig	8,000

AVERAGE TRAVEL TIME
OF SPERM TO EGG
IN VARIOUS ANIMALS

ANIMAL	TRAVEL TIME
Cow	2–3 minutes
Mouse	15 minutes
Guinea Pig	15 minutes
Pig	15 minutes
Rat	15–30 minutes
Human	5–68 minutes
Sheep	6–300 minutes
Horse	5–8 hours

TOP 10 BABY NAMES
OF THE CENTURY

BOY	1904	GIRL
William, John, George, Thomas, Arthur, James, Charles, Frederick, Albert, Ernest		Mary, Florence, Doris, Edith, Dorothy, Annie, Margaret, Alice, Elizabeth, Elsie

BOY	1914	GIRL
John, William, George, Thomas, James, Arthur, Frederick, Albert, Charles, Robert		Mary, Margaret, Doris, Dorothy, Kathleen, Florence, Elsie, Edith, Elizabeth, Winifred

BOY	1924	GIRL
John, William, George, James, Thomas, Ronald, Kenneth, Robert, Arthur, Frederick		Margaret, Mary, Joan, Joyce, Dorothy, Kathleen, Doris, Irene, Elizabeth, Eileen

BOY	1934	GIRL
John, Peter, William, Brian, David, James, Michael, Ronald, Kenneth, George		Margaret, Jean, Mary, Joan, Patricia, Sheila, Barbara, Doreen, June, Shirley

BOY	1944	GIRL
John, David, Michael, Peter, Robert, Anthony, Brian, Alan, William, James		Margaret, Patricia, Christine, Mary, Jean, Ann, Susan, Janet, Maureen, Barbara

BOY	1954	GIRL
David, John, Stephen, Michael, Peter, Robert, Paul, Alan, Christopher, Richard		Susan, Linda, Christine, Margaret, Janet, Patricia, Carol, Elizabeth, Mary, Anne

BOY	1964	GIRL
David, Paul, Andrew, Mark, John, Michael, Stephen, Ian, Robert, Richard		Susan, Julie, Karen, Jacqueline, Deborah, Tracey, Jane, Helen, Diane, Sharon

BOY	1974	GIRL
Paul, Mark, David, Andrew, Richard, Christopher, James, Simon, Michael, Matthew		Sarah, Claire, Nicola, Emma, Lisa, Joanne, Michelle, Helen, Samantha, Karen

BOY	1984	GIRL
Christopher, James, David, Daniel, Michael, Matthew, Andrew, Richard, Paul, Mark		Sarah, Laura, Gemma, Emma, Rebecca, Claire, Victoria, Samantha, Rachel, Amy

BOY	1994	GIRL
Thomas, James, Jack, Daniel, Matthew, Ryan, Joshua, Luke, Samuel, Jordan		Rebecca, Lauren, Jessica, Charlotte, Hannah, Sophie, Amy, Emily, Laura, Emma

BOY	2000	GIRL
Jack, Thomas, James, Joshua, Daniel, Harry, Samuel, Joseph, Matthew, Callum		Chloe, Emily, Megan, Charlotte, Jessica, Lauren, Sophie, Olivia, Hannah, Lucy

BOY	2003	GIRL
Jack, Joshua, Thomas, James, Daniel, Oliver, Benjamin, Samuel, William, Joseph		Emily, Ellie, Chloe, Jessica, Sophie, Megan, Lucy, Olivia, Charlotte, Hannah

FERTILE LIFE OF SPERM
IN VARIOUS ANIMALS

ANIMAL	FERTILE LIFE OF SPERM
Mouse	6 hours
Rat	14 hours
Guinea Pig	21–22 hours
Pig	24–38 hours
Human	24–48 hours
Cow	28–50 hours
Rabbit	30–32 hours
Sheep	30–48 hours
Horse	6 days
Bat	135 days

MORALS IN AESOP'S FABLES

FABLE	MORAL
The Ant and the Grasshopper	Prepare for a rainy day.
The Ant and the Chrysalis	Appearances are deceptive.
The Boy Who Cried Wolf	Liars are not believed when they tell the truth.
The Dog in the Manger	People deny others what they can't enjoy themselves.
The Eagle and the Fox	Do to others as you would have them do to you.
The Farmer and the Stork	Birds of a feather flock together.
The Father and His Sons	United we stand, divided we fall.
The Fox Who Lost His Tail	Misery loves company.
The Fox and the Goat	Look before you leap.
The Goose That Laid the Golden Eggs	Much wants more and loses all.
The Hare and the Tortoise	Slow and steady wins the race.
The Heifer and the Ox	He who laughs last laughs best.
The Man and His Two Sweethearts	Those who seek to please everyone, please no one.
Mercury and the Woodman	Honesty is the best policy.
The Milkmaid and Her Pail	Don't count your chickens before they hatch.
The North Wind and the Sun	Persuasion is better than force.
The Peacock and the Crane	Fine feathers don't make fine birds.
The Raven and the Swan	A change of habit cannot alter nature.
The Vixen and the Lioness	Quality is better than quantity.

AVERAGE U.K. NANNY SALARIES
(ACCORDING TO NANNY TAX 2004)

	AVERAGE WEEKLY SALARY	
	LIVE-IN	LIVE-OUT
London	£292	£382
Outer London & Home Counties	£267	£325
Other U.K. cities & towns	£238	£284

	ANNUAL GROSS	
	LIVE-IN	LIVE-OUT
London	£19,956	£26,937
Outer London & Home Counties	£18,007	£22,514
Other U.K. cities & towns	£15,760	£19,335

DAYS OF GESTATION
FOR VARIOUS ANIMALS

Opossum	12
Hamster	16
Mouse	21
Rabbit	31
Squirrel	44
Eagle, Golden	44
Bobcat	60
Dog	61
Cat	63
Lion	108
Pig	114
Goat	145
Sheep	150
Bear, Grizzly	220
Human	266
Cow	284
Horse	336
Sea Lion	360
Whale	360
Donkey	374
Camel	400
Giraffe	425
Rhino, Grey	480
Rhino, Black	540
Elephant, Indian	624

ANNUAL COST OF RAISING A CHILD

(EXCLUDING EDUCATION**)

| | ANNUAL COST PER CHILD | | TOTAL ANNUAL COST (in billions) | | TOTAL COST (in billions) |
	Boy	Girl	Boy	Girl	
Holidays	£668.2	£740.7	£4.54	£4.71	£9.25
Food	£606.4	£615.4	£4.12	£4.04	£8.16
Hobbies	£593.1	£500.0	£4.03	£3.23	£7.26
Clothes	£448.9	£532.5	£3.05	£3.44	£6.49
School trips	£292.9	£328.2	£1.99	£2.12	£4.11
Pocket money	£179.6	£199.7	£1.22	£1.29	£2.51
TOTAL	£2,790	£2,916	£18.95	£18.83	£37.78

This equates to roughly £47,430 for every boy and £49,572 for every girl for the first 17 years of their lives.

Source: Egg PLC, October 2004

** *According to the Independent Schools Council, the average fee for a private (non-boarding) school is £7,911 per annum.*

CHOICE OF CONTRACEPTION
BY MARITAL STATUS

(GREAT BRITAIN 2002)

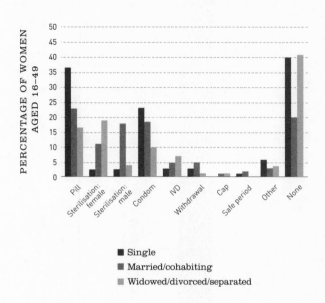

- ■ Single
- ■ Married/cohabiting
- ■ Widowed/divorced/separated

(U.K. National Statistics 'Living in Britain' 2002)

ANCIENT CHINESE BIRTH GENDER PREDICTOR

		MONTH OF CONCEPTION											
		J	F	M	A	M	J	J	A	S	O	N	D
AGE OF MOTHER	18	F	M	F	M	M	M	M	M	M	M	M	M
	19	M	F	M	F	F	M	M	F	M	M	F	F
	20	F	M	F	M	M	M	M	M	M	F	M	M
	21	M	F	F	F	F	F	F	F	F	F	F	F
	22	F	M	M	F	M	F	F	M	F	F	F	F
	23	M	M	M	F	M	M	F	F	F	M	M	F
	24	M	F	F	M	M	F	M	F	M	M	F	M
	25	F	M	F	M	F	M	F	M	F	M	M	M
	26	M	M	M	M	M	F	M	F	F	M	F	F
	27	F	F	M	M	F	M	F	F	M	F	M	M
	28	M	M	M	F	F	M	F	M	F	F	M	F
	29	F	M	F	F	M	F	F	M	F	M	F	F
	30	M	M	F	M	F	M	M	M	M	M	M	M
	31	M	M	M	M	F	F	M	F	M	F	F	F
	32	M	F	F	M	F	M	M	F	M	M	F	M
	33	F	M	M	F	F	M	F	M	F	M	M	F
	34	M	M	F	F	M	F	M	M	F	M	F	F
	35	M	F	M	F	M	F	M	F	M	M	F	M
	36	M	F	M	M	M	F	M	M	F	F	F	F
	37	F	F	M	F	F	F	M	F	M	M	F	M
	38	M	M	F	F	M	F	F	M	F	F	M	F
	39	F	F	M	F	F	F	M	F	M	M	F	M
	40	M	M	M	F	M	F	M	F	M	F	F	M
	41	F	F	M	F	M	M	F	F	M	F	M	F
	42	M	F	F	M	M	M	M	M	F	M	F	M
	43	F	M	F	F	M	M	M	F	F	F	M	M
	44	M	F	F	F	M	F	M	M	F	M	F	M
	45	F	M	F	M	F	F	M	F	M	F	M	F

SOLOMON'S WISDOM IN JUDGEMENT

I KINGS 3:16–28, NEW REVISED STANDARD VERSION

Later, two women who were prostitutes came to the king and stood before him. The one woman said, 'Please, my lord, this woman and I live in the same house; and I gave birth while she was in the house. Then on the third day after I gave birth, this woman also gave birth. We were together; there was no one else with us in the house, only the two of us were in the house. Then this woman's son died in the night, because she lay on top of him. She got up in the night and took my son from beside me while your servant slept. She laid him at her breast, and laid her dead son at my breast. When I rose in the morning to nurse my son, I saw that he was dead; but when I looked at him closely in the morning, clearly it was not the son I had borne.' But the other woman said, 'No, the living son is mine, and the dead son is yours.' The first said, 'No, the dead son is yours, and the living son is mine.' So they argued before the king.

Then the king said, 'The one says, "This is my son that is alive, and your son is dead"; while the other says, "Not so! Your son is dead, and my son is the living one."' So the king said, 'Bring me a sword,' and they brought a sword before the king. The king said, 'Divide the living boy in two; then give half to the one, and half to the other.' But the woman whose son was alive said to the king – because compassion for her son burned within her – 'Please, my lord, give her the living boy; certainly do not kill him!' The other said, 'It shall be neither mine nor yours; divide it.' Then the king responded: 'Give the first woman the living boy; do not kill him. She is his mother.' All Israel heard the judgement that the king had rendered; and they stood in awe of the king, because they perceived that the wisdom of God was in him, to execute justice.

HOW TO TELL FROM A SONOGRAM
IF YOU'RE HAVING A BOY OR A GIRL

View from underneath: The buttocks are on the right, the thighs are pointing left. The short line between the thighs is the penis. It's a boy!

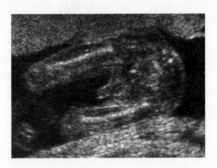

View from underneath: The buttocks are on the left, the thighs are pointing right. The three horizontal stripes between the legs are the labia folds and clitoris. It's a girl!

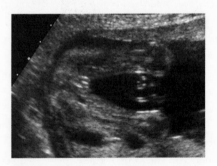

CHILD RULERS

King Tutankhamen (1370–1352 B.C.) Crowned king of Egypt from age nine. Married his half-sister, Cleopatra.

Alexander Severus (222–235) Crowned emperor by the Roman army at age thirteen. His mother accompanied him to the battlefield, and both were murdered in their camp by soldiers.

Louis the Child (893–911) Crowned king of Germany at age six.

Henri VI (1421–1471) Crowned king of England at age of nine months and king of France at ten months. Murdered in the Tower of London.

Mary Queen of Scots (1542–1587) Ascended the throne at the age of seven days.

James VI of Scotland (1566–1625) Crowned king of Scotland at the age of one year and one month.

Daudi Chwa (1893–1942) Crowned king of Buganda (today Uganda) at age four.

Emperor Pu Yi (1906–1967) Ascended the Chinese throne at age three. Resigned at age five. Restored at age nine, but lasted only six days. Known as the Last Emperor.

King Oyo Nyimba Kabamba Iguru Rukidi IV (B. 1992–) Crowned king of Toro, a kingdom in Uganda, at age three.

Gregor Mendel (Austrian botanist and monk, 1822–1884) laid the groundwork for genetics by discovering that specific traits are carried on specific *genes*. Some traits have only two possible gene types, or *alleles* – a dominant allele and a recessive one. If a plant or animal possesses two identical alleles, it is said to be *homologous*, and if it possesses two different genes is called *heterozygous*. The classic example is to assume a dominant G represents green-colored peas and a recessive g represents yellow-colored peas. A pea with GG genes is green, a pea with Gg genes is also green, and a pea with gg genes is yellow. The following chart, called a *Punnett square*, shows the possible offspring from two parents with heterozygous genes.

	G	g
G	GG	Gg
g	Gg	gg

SOME FIRST EDITION CHILDREN'S STORIES
AND THEIR VALUES

Charlotte's Web by E. B. White. NY: 1952.
In dust jacket. £420

Madeline by Ludwig Bemelmans. NY: 1939.
In dust jacket. £420

The Lion, The Witch and the Wardrobe by C. S. Lewis.
London: 1950. In dust jacket. £520

Eloise by Kay Thompson. NY: 1955. In dust jacket. £780

The Cat in the Hat by Theodor Giesel. NY: 1957.
In dust jacket with 200/200 price on flap. £4,000

The Velveteen Rabbit, or How Toys Become Real
by Margery Williams Bianco. London: 1922.
In dust jacket. £5,200

The Wonderful Wizard of Oz by L. Frank Baum.
Chicago & NY: 1900. £6,500

Alice in Wonderland by Charles Dodgson
(Lewis Carroll). London: 1866. £7,800

The Hobbit by J. R. R. Tolkien. London: 1937.
In dust jacket. £10,500

The Wind in the Willows by Kenneth Grahame.
London: 1908. In dust jacket. £13,000

Account of a Visit from St. Nicholas [*The Night
Before Christmas*] by Clement C. Moore. Philadelphia:
1825. In the United States National Almanac
by David M'Clure. £21,000

The Tale of Peter Rabbit by Beatrix Potter. London:
Privately printed, December 1901. One of 250. £26,000

The Book of Nonsense by Edward Lear. London:
Thomas M'Lean, 1846. One of seven surviving
copies. £26,000

NAMES OF YOUNG IN VARIOUS SPECIES

Alligator: *hatchling*

Alpaca: *cria*

Ant: *antling*

Ape: *baby, infant*

Baboon: *infant*

Bee: *larva*

Beetle: *grub, mealworm*

Boar: *calf, farrow, piglet*

Butterfly: *caterpillar, chrysalis, pupa*

Camel: *calf, colt, foal*

Cat: *kitten*

Cattle: *calf, stirk*

Chimpanzee: *infant*

Cicada: *nymph*

Clam: *chiton, littleneck*

Cock: *cockerel*

Cod: *codling, hake, scrod, sprag, sprat*

Cockroach: *larva, nymph*

Crane: *chick, craneling*

Crocodile: *crocklet*

Deer: *calf, kid, fawn*

Dinosaur: *hatchling, juvenile*

Dog: *puppy, whelp*

Dolphin: *calf, pup*

Dove: *squab*

Duck: *duckling, flapper*

Eagle: *eaglet, fledgling*

Echinda: *puggle*

Eel: *fly, elver*

Ewe: *teg*

Fish: *alevin, fingerling, fry*

Fly: *maggot, grub*

Fox: *cub, kit, pup*

Frog: *froglet, polliwog, tadpole*

Goat: *kid*

Goose: *gosling*

Gorilla: *infant*

Grouse: *cheeper, chick*

Guinea fowl: *keet*

Hag moth: *monkey slug*

Hare: *leveret*

Hawk: *eyas, brancher*

Hedgehog: *piglet, pup*

Hen: *pullet*

Herring: *brit, sprat*

Hog: *farrow, shoat, piglet*

Horse: *colt, filly, pony*

Hyrax: *bunny*

Jellyfish: *ephyna*

Kangaroo: *joey*

Koala: *joey*

Lemur: *infant*

Lion: *cub, lionet, shelp*

Llama: *cria*

Louse: *nit*

Mackerel: *blinker, spike, tinker*

Mink: *cub, kit*

Monkey: *infant, suckling*

Mosquito: *wiggler, wriggler*

Mouse: *kitten, pinkie*

Otter: *pup, whelp*

Ox: *calf, stot*

Owl: *owlet, howlet*

Oyster: *brood, spat*

Partridge: *cheeper, chick*

Pig: *farrow, piglet, pigling, shoat*

Pigeon: *nestling, squab, squeaker*

Pike: *sardine*

Possum: *joey*

Quail: *cheeper, chick, squealer*

Quokka: *joey*

Rabbit: *bunny, leveret, nestling*

Rat: *kitten, nestling, pinkie, pup*

Salmon: *alevin, fry, parr, skegger, smolt*

Scorpion: *instar*

Seal: *bachelor, beach weaner, whelp*

Sheep: *cosset, hog, lamp, lambling, teg*

Skunk: *kit, kitten*

Snake: *snakelet*

Sow: *gilt, piglet*

Springbok: *fawn*

Squirrel: *kit, kitten, nestling, pup*

Swallowtail butterfly: *orange dog*

Swan: *cygnet, flapper*

Tasmanian devil: *joey*

Toad: *tadpole*

Trout: *fingerling, fry*

Turkey: *chick, poult*

Turtle: *hatchling*

Vicuna: *cria*

Wolf: *cub, pup, whelp*

Wombat: *joey*

A VERY BRIEF GUIDE TO
IN-UTERO DEVELOPMENT

ZYGOTE: 0–40 HOURS

Cleavage divisions.

MORULA: 40 HOURS TO 4 DAYS

Reaches uterus; embryonic cell mass develops.

BLASTOCYST: 4–8 DAYS

Development of two-layer disc; implantation begins; embryonic membranes start to develop.

EMBRYO, EARLY: 12–13 DAYS

Implantation complete.

14 DAYS

Mature placenta begins to develop.

15–20 DAYS

Development of three-layer disc; neural tube begins to form; disc becomes attached to uterine wall by short, thick umbilical cord; placenta develops rapidly.

21–28 DAYS

Eyes begin to form; heart starts beating; crown-to-rump length 5 mm; growth rate about 1 mm per day; neural tube closes; vascular system develops; placental maternal-embryonic circulation begins.

EMBRYO, LATE: 5 WEEKS

Arm and leg buds form.

7 WEEKS

Facial structures fuse.

8 WEEKS

Crown-to-rump length 3 cm; weight 1 g; major development of organs completed; most external features recognisable at birth present.

FOETUS: 8–12 WEEKS

Arms and legs move; startle and sucking reflexes; facial expressions and external sex organs appear; fingerprints develop; respiratory and excretory systems develop but not functional; laguno develops.

13–16 WEEKS

Skin and true hair develop; skeleton becomes bony.

17–24 WEEKS

Length 20 cm; weight 450 g; movements become obvious to mother; old cells discarded and replaced by new cells, hence cells in amniotic fluid.

25–28 WEEKS

Begins to acquire subcutaneous fat; terminals of lungs and blood vessels develop.

BY 38 WEEKS

Foetus becomes plump, laguno sheds, testes of male descend.

BASIC FERTILISATION

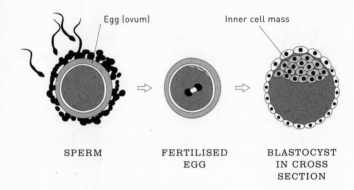

Egg (ovum)   Inner cell mass

SPERM   FERTILISED
EGG

BLASTOCYST
IN CROSS
SECTION

AGE OF PATERNITY,
ACCORDING TO THE BIBLE

Adam *begat* Seth	130
Seth *begat* Enos	109
Enos *begat* Ca-i'nan	90
Ca-i'nan *begat* Mahal'aleel	70
Mahal'aleel *begat* Jared	65
Jared *begat* Enoch	162
Enoch *begat* Methu'selah	65
Methu'selah *begat* Lamech	187
Lamech *begat* Noah	182
Noah *begat* Shem, Ham and Japheth	500
Shem *begat* Arphaxad	100
Arphaxad *begat* Salah	530
Salah *begat* Eber	30
Eber *begat* Peleg	430
Peleg *begat* Reu	30
Reu *begat* Serug	230
Serug *begat* Nahor	30
Nahor *begat* Terah	920
Terah *begat* Abram, Nahor and Haran	70
Abram *begat* Isaac	100
Isaac *begat* Jacob and Esau	60

SOME FAMOUS VOICES
IN ANIMATED FILMS

FILM	CHARACTERS	FAMOUS ACTOR VOICE
Aladdin	Genie	Robin Williams
The Aristocats	Duchess	Eva Gabor
Beauty and the Beast	Lumière	Jerry Orbach
	Mrs Potts	Angela Lansbury
A Bug's Life	Princess Atta	Julia Louis-Dreyfus
	Hopper	Kevin Spacey
	The Queen	Phyllis Diller
	Francis	Dennis Leary
The Emperor's New Groove	Kuzco	David Spade
	Yzma	Eartha Kitt
	Pacha	John Goodman
Finding Nemo	Marlin	Albert Brooks
	Dory	Ellen DeGeneres
The Fox and the Hound	Tod (adult)	Mickey Rooney
	Copper (young)	Corey Feldman
	Copper (adult)	Kurt Russell
	Vixey	Sandy Duncan
The Hunchback of Notre Dame	Esmeralda	Demi Moore
	Quasimodo	Tom Hulce
	Phoebus	Kevin Kline
	Hugo	Jason Alexander
The Jungle Book	King Louie	Louis Prima
	Baloo	Phil Harris
	Shere Khan	George Sanders

FILM	CHARACTERS	FAMOUS ACTOR VOICE
Lady and the Tramp	Darling, Si, Am, Peg	Peggy Lee
The Lion King	Simba (young)	Jonathan Taylor Thomas
	Simba (adult)	Matthew Broderick
	Mufasa	James Earl Jones
	Scar	Jeremy Irons
	Timon	Nathan Lane
	Rafiki	Robert Guillaume
	Shenzi	Whoopi Goldberg
The Great Mouse Detective	Professor Ratigan	Vincent Price
Monsters, Inc.	James 'Sulley' Sullivan	John Goodman
	Mike Wazowski	Billy Crystal
	Celia	Meg Tilly
	Randall Boggs	Steve Buscemi
Mulan	Mushu	Eddie Murphy
Pocahontas	Captain John Smith	Mel Gibson
	Thomas	Christian Bale
The Rescuers Down Under	Bernard	Bob Newhart
	Bianca	Eva Gabor
	Wilbur	John Candy
Toy Story	Woody	Tom Hanks
	Buzz Lightyear	Tim Allen
	Mr Potato Head	Don Rickles
	Hamm	John Ratzenberger

HOW TO PREDICT OVULATION
WITHOUT A KIT

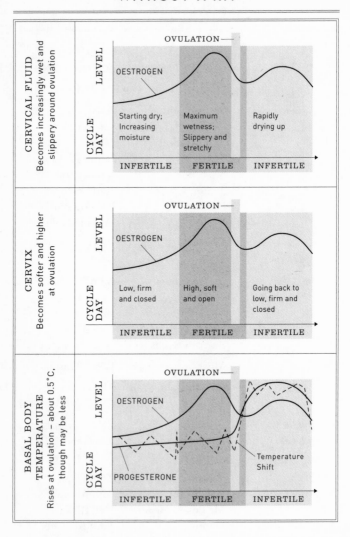

FAMILY CHANGES IN GREAT BRITAIN

FAMILIES WITH DEPENDENT CHILDREN BY FAMILY TYPE

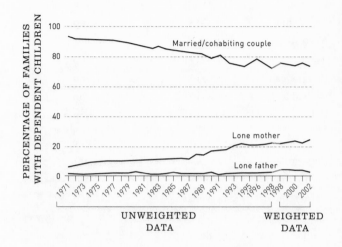

(U.K. national Statistics, 2002 General Household Survey)

MATERNITY BENEFITS
AROUND THE WORLD

COUNTRY	LENGTH OF LEAVE	% OF WAGES
Algeria	14 weeks	100
Argentina	90 days	100
Australia	1 year	0
Austria	16 weeks	100
Bangladesh	12 weeks	100
Barbados	12 weeks	100
Bolivia	60 days	100 of minimum wage + 70% above
Botswana	12 weeks	25
Cambodia	90 days	50
Cameroon	14 weeks	100
Canada	17–18 weeks	55 for 15 weeks
China	90 days	100
Congo	14 weeks	67
Côte d'Ivoire	14 weeks	100
Cuba	18 weeks	100
El Salvador	12 weeks	75
Egypt	50 days	100
Ethiopia	90 days	100
Fiji	84 days	Flat rate
France	16–26 weeks	100
Hungary	24 weeks	100
India	12 weeks	100

COUNTRY	LENGTH OF LEAVE	% OF WAGES
Iran	90 days	66.7 for 16 weeks
Italy	5 months	80
Japan	14 weeks	60
Kuwait	70 days	100
Israel	12 weeks	75
Libya	50 days	50
Luxembourg	16 weeks	100
Mexico	12 weeks	100
Morocco	12 weeks	100
Namibia	12 weeks	As prescribed
Panama	14 weeks	100
Russia	140 days	100
Rwanda	12 weeks	67
Solomon Islands	12 weeks	25
South Africa	12 weeks	45
Spain	16 weeks	100
Sri Lanka	12 weeks	100
Sudan	8 weeks	100
Turkey	12 weeks	66.7
Ukraine	126 days	100
United Kingdom	14–18 weeks	90 for 6 weeks, flat rate after
United States	12 weeks	0

Two structures are present in the foetal heart that disappear shortly after birth: the patent ductus arteriosus, a blood vessel between the aorta and pulmonary artery, and the patent formen ovale, the opening between the right and left atria. These are needed because the placenta, not the foetal lungs, supplies oxygen to foetal blood.

IVC = inferior vena cava
SVC = superior vena cava
PV = pulmonary vein
RA = right atrium
LA = left atrium
PFO = patent formen ovale
TV = tricuspid valve
MV = mitral valve
RV = right ventricle
LV = left ventricle
PA = pulmonary artery
MPA = main pulmonary artery
RPA = right pulmonary artery
LPA = left pulmonary artery
Ao = aorta
AAo = ascending aorta
DAo = descending aorta
PDA = patent ductus arteriosus

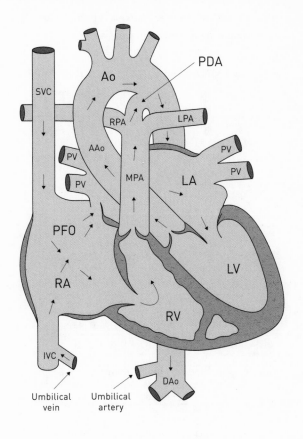

BLOOD TYPES

Each child has two alleles, one from each parent. Blood types A and B have codominant alleles; O is recessive.

ALLELE COMBINATIONS	BLOOD TYPES
OO	O
AO	A
BO	B
AB	AB
AA	A
BB	B

Therefore:

Blood type of the child:

	CHILD →	AND THE FATHER IS:			
		A	B	AB	O
IF THE MOTHER IS:	A	A or O	A, B, AB, O	A, B, AB, O	A or O
	B	A, B, AB, O	B or O	A, B, AB, O	B or O
	AB	A, B, AB, O	A, B, O	A, B, AB	A or B
	O	A or O	B or O	A or B	O

Blood type of the father:

	FATHER →	AND THE CHILD IS:			
		A	B	AB	O
IF THE MOTHER IS:	A	A, B, AB, O	B or AB	B or AB	A, B, O
	B	A or AB	A, B, AB, O	A or AB	A, B, O
	AB	A, B, AB, O	A, B, AB, O	A, B, AB	Not possible
	O	A or B	B or AB	Not possible	A, B, O

GRIM FATES IN
GRIMMS' FAIRY TALES

FAIRY TALE	VILLAIN	FATE
Tom Thumb	Wolf	Disembowelled with knives and scissors by Tom's parents.
Hansel & Gretel	Witch	Burnt to death in her own oven.
Little Red Riding Hood	Wolf	Cut open by huntsman and skinned.
Snow White	Queen	Forced to put on red-hot iron slippers and dance until she died.
Rumplestiltskin	Rumplestiltskin	Tore himself in two in rage.
The Wolf and Seven Young Kids	Wolf	Cut open, stuffed with rocks, stitched up and drowned.
Cinderella	Stepsisters	Eyes pecked out by pigeons.
The Goose Girl	The princess's waiting maid	Stripped naked, placed in barrel studded with nails and dragged by white horses.
The Six Swans	Mother-in-law	Bound to a stake and burnt to ashes.

THE HUMAN PLACENTA

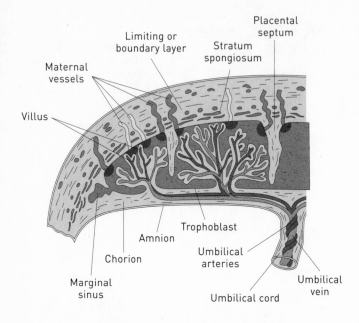

The placenta connects the foetus to the uterine wall, and is the means by which the foetus's nutritive, respiratory and excretory needs are carried out. Both foetal and maternal blood traverse the placenta. Foetal blood flows up through the *umbilical artery* into very fine blood vessels called *placental villi*. These are bathed in maternal blood in the *intervillous space*. Through the walls of the villi, the foetal blood absorbs oxygen and nutrition, and gives up waste. The foetal blood, thus purified, then flows back to the foetus through the *umbilical vein*.

THE FINEST STRIPES
A NEWBORN CAN SEE
FROM 30 CENTIMETRES AWAY

MAJOR NEWBORN REFLEXES

NAME	TESTING METHOD	RESPONSE	COURSE
BLINK	Light flash	Closing both eyelids	Permanent
BICEPS REFLEX	Tap on the tendon of the biceps muscle	Short contraction of the biceps muscle	In first few days it is brisker than later
KNEE JERK OR PATELLAR TENDON REFLEX	Tap on the tendon below the patella, or kneecap	Quick extension or kick of the knee	More pronounced in first 2 days than later
BABINSKI	Gentle stroking of side of the infant's foot from heel to toes	Dorsal flexion of the big toe; extension of the other toes	Usually disappears near the end of the first year; replaced by plantar flexion of big toe in normal adult
WITHDRAWAL REFLEX	Pinprick is applied to the sole of the infant's foot	Leg flexion	Constantly present in the first 10 days; present but less intense later
PLANTAR OR TOE GRASP	Pressure applied with finger against the balls of feet	Plantar flexion of all toes	Disappears in 8 to 12 months
PALMAR OR AUTOMATIC HAND GRASP	A rod or finger is pressed against infant's palm	Infant grasps object	Increases during the first month; disappears in 3 to 4 months; replaced by voluntary grasp at 4 and 5 months

MAJOR NEWBORN REFLEXES *continued*

NAME	TESTING METHOD	RESPONSE	COURSE
MORO REFLEX	Sudden loud or jarring sound (for example, bang on the table) or baby is dropped onto bed to elicit startle	Arms thrown out, then brought towards each other convulsively; hands fanned then clinched; spine and lower extremities extended	Disappears in 6 to 7 months
STEPPING	Baby supported upright; examiner moves the infant forwards and tilts to one side	Rhythmic stepping movements	Disappears in 3 to 5 months
ROOTING REFLEX	Cheek stimulated by light pressure from finger	Baby turns head and tries to suck finger	Disappears in 3 to 4 months
SUCKING RESPONSE	Index finger inserted about 3 to 4 cm into mouth	Rhythmic sucking	Sucking less intensive and regular during the first 3 to 4 days
BABKIN OR PALMOMENTAL REFLEX	Pressure applied on both palms when baby lying on back	Mouth opens, eyes close and head turns to midline	Disappears in 3 to 4 months

TOY OF THE YEAR, 1965-2004

ACCORDING TO THE TOY RETAILERS' ASSOCIATION

1965	James Bond Aston Martin die-cast car
1966	Action Man
1967	Spirograph
1968	Sindy
1969	Hot Wheels cars
1970	Sindy
1971	Katie Kopykat writing doll
1972	Plasticraft modelling kits
1973	Mastermind—board game
1974	Lego Family set
1975	Lego Basic set
1976	Peter Powell kites
1977	Playmobil Playpeople
1978	Combine Harvester (Britains)
1979	Legoland Space kits
1980	Rubik's Cube
1981	Rubik's Cube
1982	Star Wars
1983	Star Wars toys
1984	Masters of the Universe
1985	Transformers (Optimus Prime)
1986	Transformers (Optimus Prime)
1987	Sylvanian Families
1988	Sylvanian Families
1989	Sylvanian Families
1990	Teenage Mutant Ninja Turtles

1991	Nintendo Game Boy
1992	WWF Wrestlers
1993	Thunderbird's Tracey Island
1994	Power Rangers
1995	POGS
1996	Barbie
1997	Teletubbies
1998	Furby
1999	Furby Babies
2000	Teksta
2001	Bionicles
2002	Beyblades
2003	Beyblades
2004	Robosapien

MEDIAN MONTHLY INTERVAL
FROM MARRIAGE TO FIRST BIRTH,
IN ENGLAND AND WALES

YEAR	WOMEN MARRIED ONLY ONCE	REMARRIED WOMEN
1975	28	15
1976	29	17
1977	29	18
1978	31	18
1979	30	17
1980	29	16
1981	28	17
1982	29	18
1983	29	19
1984	29	18
1985	28	17
1986	27	16
1987	27	16
1988	27	15
1989	27	16
1990	27	16
1991	28	17
1992	28	17
1993	29	16
1994	28	18
1995	29	18
1996	28	17
1997	28	18
1998	27	17
1999	27	17
2000	26	18
2001	27	18

CHILD SHOE SIZES

To determine shoe size, measure the bare foot from the heel to the end of the longest toe.

U.S.	U.K.	EUROPE	CENTIMETRES
0	0	15	8
1	0	16–16.5	9
2	1	17	10
3	2	17.5–18.5	10.5
4	3	19–20	11.5
5	4	20–21	12.5
6	5	21.5–22.5	13
7	6	23–24	14
8	7	24–25	15
9	8	25.5–26	15.5
10	9	26.5–27.5	16.5
11	10	27.5–28.5	17.5
12	11	29–30	18

YOGA POSE TO RELIEVE SHOULDER PAIN
FROM CARRYING AN INFANT

Garudasana, or Eagle Pose

1. Stand with arms and legs straight. Bend knees slightly. Lift left foot. Cross left thigh over right. Point left toes, press foot back and hook top of foot behind right calf.

2. Stretch arms straight forwards, parallel to the floor, and spread scapulas wide across the back. Cross arms in front so that right arm is above left. Bend elbows. Fit right elbow into the crook of left, and raise forearms perpendicular to floor.

3. Press hands together with palms facing. The thumb of right hand should pass in front of little finger of left. Lift elbows, and stretch fingers towards ceiling.

4. Repeat with arms and legs reversed.

SLANG TERMS
FOR PREGNANCY

Preggers

Up the duff

Bun in the oven

With child

In a bad way

In the family way

Knocked up

Banjaxed

In the club

In the pudding club

Up the spout

Reduced minerals whey, vegetable oils, skimmed milk powder, lactose, emulsifiers (soya lecithin and monoglycerides of fatty acids), calcium chloride, potassium bicarbonate, sodium citrate, vitamin C, taurine, potassium hydroxide, ferrous sulphate, potassium citrate, zinc sulphate, cytidine-5'-monophosphate, calcium hydroxide, disodium uridine-5'-monophosphate, vitamin E, antioxidant, (tocopherol-rich extract), adenosine-5'-monophosphate, niacin, disodium inosine-5'- monophosphate, disodium guanosine-5'-monophosphate, pantothenic acid, vitamin A, copper sulphate, potassium chloride, thiamine, vitamin B6, riboflavin, beta-carotene, manganese sulphate, folic acid, potassium iodide, vitamin K, sodium selenite, biotin, vitamin D, vitamin B12

APPROXIMATE COMPOSITION OF HUMAN COLOSTRUM, HUMAN MILK AND COW'S MILK (PER DL)

	HUMAN COLOSTRUM	HUMAN MILK	COW'S MILK
COMPONENTS			
Water (g)	87	87	87
Total solids (g)	13	13	13
Protein (g)	7.9	1.1	3.5
Fat (g)	1.3	4.5	3.7
Lactose (g)	3.2	6.8	4.9
Ash, or mineral content (g)	0.6	0.2	0.7
PROTEINS (% OF TOTAL PROTEIN)			
Casein	—	40	82
Whey protein	—	60	18
MAJOR WHEY PROTEINS (MG)			
Lactalbumin	333	263	40
Lactoferrin	384	168	—
Lysozyme	34	42	—
Albumin	36	52	23
IgA	364	142	40
MINERALS (MG)			
Na	92	15	58
K	55	55	138
Cl	117	43	103
Ca	31	33	125
Mg	4	4	12
P	14	15	100
Fe	0.09	0.15	0.10
VITAMINS (MG)			
A	89	53	34
C	4,400	4,300	1,600
D	0.1	0.03	0.06
Riboflavin	30	43	157
Nicotinic acid	75	172	85
Thiamine	15	16	42

NAMES OF 'DR. SEUSS' CHARACTERS

Aaron (an alligator), Abigail, Aldermen, Alice (a Hooded Klopfer), Aunt Ada, Aunt Annie, Australian fish, Beagle-Beaked-Bald-Headed Grinch, Beft, Bell ringer, Bellar, Ben, Better Hunch, Benjamin B Bicklebaum, Biffer-Baum Birds, Billy Billings, Bim, Bingle Bug, Bippo-No-Bungus, Birthday Honk-Honker, Blindfolded Bowman from Brigger-ba-Root, Pinner Blinn, Blogg, Bloogs, Bofa, Bolster, Bombastic Aghast, Pete Briggs, Brown Bar-ba-loots, Brutus (a horse), Bumble-Tub Club, Captain of the Guards, Cat in the Hat, Catfish, Chief Yookeroo, Chief-in-charge-of-fish, Chippendale Mupp, Chuggs, Circus Fish, Clark, Clover (a horse), Collapsible Frink, Soapy Cooper, Bartholomew Cubbins, Curious Crandalls, Dad, Dake, Daniel (the Kick-a-Poo Spaniel), Dapples (a horse), Dawf, Dellar, Dinn, Diver Getz, Diver Gitz, Dog Fish, David Donald Doo, Down Hunch, Dr. Ballew, Dr. Blinn, Dr. Derring's Singing Herrings, Dr. Diller, Dr. Drew, Dr. Fitzgerald, Dr. Fitzpatrick, Dr. Fitzsimmons, Dr. Fonz, Dr. Ginns, Dr. McGrew, Dr. McGuire, Dr. McPherson, Dr. Pollen, Dr. Schmidt, Dr. Sinatra, Dr. Smoot, Dr. Spreckles, Dr. Sylvester, Dr. Timpkins, Dr. Tompkins, Dr. Van Ness, Dr. Von Eiffel, Donald Driscoll Drew, Drum-tummied Snumm, Dutter and Dutter (cake cutters), East Beast, Ed, Eric, Eskimo Fish, Executioner, Farmer, Father of Nadd, Father of the Father of Nadd, Fibbel, Fiffer-feffer-feff, Findow, Finney, Fish, Fizza-ma-wizza-ma-dill, Flannel-Wing Jay, Floob-Boober-Bab-Boober-Bubs, Flummox, Flunnel, Flustard, Foo-Foo the Snoo, Foon, Foona-Lagoona Baboona, Four-Way Hunch, Fox, Fred, Fritz, Fuddnudler

Brothers (Bipper, Bud, Skipper, Jipper, Jeffrey, Jud, Horatio, Horace, Hendrix, Hud, Dinwoodie, Dinty, Dud, Fitzsimmon, Frederick, Fud, Slinky, Stinkey, Stuart, Stud, Lud), Funicular Goats, Fredric Futzenfall, Gack, Gasket, Geeling, Gellar, George, Ghair, Gherkin, Glikker, Glotz: the Glunk, Arabella Godiva, Gussie Godiva, Hedwig Godiva Lulu, Godiva, Mitzi Godiva, Teenie Godiva, Goo-Goose, Gootch, Gox, Grand Duke Wilfred, Grandpa, Great Birthday Bird, Grice, Grickily Gractus, Grinch, Grizzly-Ghastly, Grox, Guff, Gusset, Ham-ikka-Schnim-ikka-Schnam-ikka-Schnopp, Happy Hunch, Harp-Twanging Snarp, Herk-Heimer Sisters, Herman (a squirrel), High Gargel-orum, Hilda Hen, Hinkle-Horn Honkers, Hippo-Heimers, Homework Hunch, Hoodwink, Hooey (a parrot), Peter T. Hooper, Hopp-Soup-Snoop Group, Horton the Elephant, Huffle, Humming-Fish, Humpf-Humpf-a-Dumpfer, Ichabod, Iota, Ish, It-Kutch, Itch-a-pods, Jake the Pillow Snake, Jedd, Jeronimo, Jertain, Jibboo, Jill-ikka-Jast, Jim, Jimbo Jones (a jellyfish), Jo-Jo, Josts, Joe, Jogg-oons, Jerry Jordan, Juggling Jott, Blooie Katz, Chooie Katz, Fooie Katz, Kooie Katz, Looie, King of Katzen-Stein Katz, Prooie Katz, Zooie Katzen-bein, King Birtram, King Derwin of Didd, King's Magicians, Katy Klopps, Klotz, Mr. and Mrs. J. Carmichael Knox, Nixie Knox, Knox, Kitty O'Sullivan Krauss, Kweet, Kwigger, Lass-a-Jack, Little Cats A-Z, Liz, Lolla-Lee-Lou, Long-Legger Kwong, Little Lola Lopp, Lorax, Lord Droon, Lord Godiva, Luke Luck, Lunks, Lurch, Mack the Turtle, Marco, Max (a dog), Mayor of Who-Ville, Mayor,

Mayzie Bird, Sylvester McMonkey McBean, Dave McCave (all 23 of them), Mike McCobb, Gertrude McFuzz, Gerald McGrew, Morris McGurk, Snorter and His Snore-a-Snort Band McPhail, Mike, Miss Becker, Miss Fuddle-dee-Duddle, Marvin K. Mooney, Mop-Noodled Finch, Moth-Watching Sneth, Mr. Brown, Mr. Glotz, Mr. Gump, Mr. Sneelock, Mrs. Brown, Mrs. Kangaroo and child, Mrs. McCave, Mrs. Umbroso, Mt. Strookoo Cuckoo, Mulligatawny, Munch Hunch, Nadd, Natch, Nathan (a war horse), Nazzim of Bazzim, Ned, Nellar, Nerd, Nerkle, Nink, Nizzards (black birds), Nolster, Nook Gase, Nook, Nooth Grush, North-Going Zax, Norval, Nupboard, Nureau, Nutch, Conrad Cornelius O'Donald O'Dell, Obsk, Ogler, the Onceler, Pam the Clam, Papa, Parsifal (a horse), Pat, Patrol Cats, Peeping Dick, Peeping Drexel, Peeping Frelinghuysen, Peeping Harry, Peeping Jack, Peeping Tom, Pelf, Peter the Postman, Plain-Belly Sneetches, Pop, Preep, Proo, Pup, Quandary, Quincy Queek, Queen of Quincy, Quilligan quail, Quimney, Quiz-Docs, Real Tough Hunch, Red, Jo Red-Zoff, Mo Red-Zoff, Right-Side-Up Song Girls, Rink-Rinker-Fink, Rolf the Walrus, Rosy Robin Ross, Royal Coachman, Royal Cook, Royal Fiddlers, Royal Laundress, Royal Trumpeter, Ruffle-Necked Sala-ma-goox, Russian Palooski, Ruthie, Sally, Sam I Am, Santa Claus, Gen. Genghis Khan Schmitz, Schanck, Sea Horse, Seersucker, Sgt. Mulvaney, Shade-Roosting Quail, Simon Sneath (a snail), Single-File Zummzian Zuks, Sir Alaric (keeper of the King's Records), Sir Beers, Sir Bopps, Sir Dawkins, Sir Hawkins, Sir Hector, Sir Jawks, Sir Jeers,

Sir Snipps, Sir Vector, Sister, Skipper Zipp, Skrink, Skritz, Silly
Sammy Slick, Slow Joe Crow, Smiling Sam (a crocodile),
Sneedle, Sneetches, Dr. Sam Snell, Snuvs, Soobrian Snipe, Sour
Hunch, South-Going Zax, South-West-Facing Cranes, Hunch
Spazzim, Sally Spingel Spungel Sporn, Spotted Atrocious,
Spritz, Star-Belly Sneetches, Stroodel, Sue, Super Hunch,
Swomee-Swans, Ted Tellar, Thidwick (a horse), Thidwick the
Moose, Thing One, Thing Two, Thing, Thing-a-ma-Jigger,
Thnadners, Through-horns-jumping Deer, Thwerll, Tick-tack-
toe, Time-Telling Fish, Tizzle-Topped Grouse, Tizzy, To-an-
Fro Marchers, Tree-Spider, Truffle, Tufted Mazurka, Twiddler
Owl, Umbus, Uncle Terwilliger, Uncle Ubb, Up Hunch, Van
Itch, Van Vleck, Very Odd Hunch, Vera Violet Vinn, Vipper of
Vipp, Vlad-i-koff, Vlad (a black-bottom eagle), Von Crandall,
Gretchen von Schwinn, Vrooms, Vug, Wasket, Willy Waterloo,
Wellar, West Beast, Whelden the Wheeler, Little Cindy-Lou
Who, Who-Bubs, Wickersham Brothers, Warren Wiggins,
Waldo Wilberforce, Will, Wily Walloo, Wocket, Wogs,
Waldo Woo, Woset, Wumbus, Wump, Yekko, Yeoman of
the Bowmen, Yeps, Yertle the Turtle, Ying, Yink, Yookie-
Ann Sue, Yooks, Yop, Yolanda Yorgenson, Yot, Yottle, Yuzz-a-
ma-Tuzz, Zable, Zall, Zamp, Zans, Zatz-it, Zax, Zeds, Zeep,
Zelf, Zellar, Ziff, Zillow, Zinn-a-Zu Bird, Zizzer-zazzer-zuzz,
Zlock, Zong, Zooks, Zoop-a-Zoop Troupe, Zower, Zuff,
Zummers

FERTILITY RATES BY AGE
IN ENGLAND & WALES

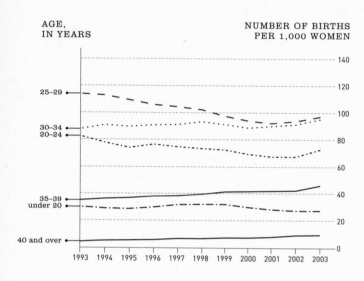

AGE,
IN YEARS

NUMBER OF BIRTHS
PER 1,000 WOMEN

25–29

30–34
20–24

35–39
under 20

40 and over

140

120

100

80

60

40

20

0

1993 1994 1995 1996 1997 1998 1999 2000 2001 2002 2003

CHANCES OF HAVING
A MULTIPLE BIRTH

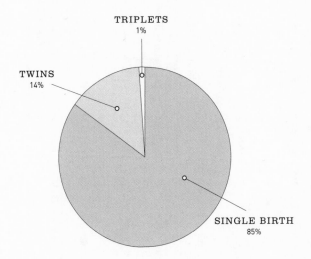

TRIPLETS
1%

TWINS
14%

SINGLE BIRTH
85%

(2001 U.K. National Statistics)

PRIMER FOR A GOOD BEDTIME STORY

THIS CHART IS BASED ON CLASSIC HERO/HEROINE ADVENTURE STORIES, SUCH AS 'STAR WARS'

CLASSIC HERO'S JOURNEY	FUNCTION	SAMPLE BEDTIME STORY
World of Common Day	Hero at home.	Girl goes to sleep.
Call to Adventure	Hero presented with a problem or challenge.	Girl wakes up in the dark and wants ice cream, but is scared of monsters.
Refusal of the Call	Hero scared to take on challenge.	Girl decides downstairs is too dark and scary.
Supernatural Aid/ Mentor	Hero receives guidance or equipment.	Girl sees her dog, who tells her that downstairs is really fun at night, and that the monsters aren't so bad.
Crossing the First Threshold	Hero finally commits to adventure.	Girl rides on dog's back to the stairs.
Tests, Allies and Enemies	Hero encounters new trials.	On stairs, girl is scared by the cat, and then by the weird noises of trees blowing against the house, and then by lightning outside. But she keeps going.

	Continues → → → →	
CLASSIC HERO'S JOURNEY	FUNCTION	SAMPLE BEDTIME STORY
Approach to the Inmost Cave	Hero on the edge of a dangerous place.	Down the long hall towards the kitchen, girl thinks she hears a monster in the study.
Supreme Ordeal	Hero in direct confrontation with greatest fear appears to die.	So girl tiptoes back through the dining room, gets a spoon, pulls a chair over to the freezer and grabs the ice cream.
Seizing the Sword	Hero takes possession of the treasure, cause to celebrate.	But girl slips as she tries to get down. As she recovers the ice cream and spoon, she hears a monster coming towards her!
The Road Back	Hero has to deal with consequences of Supreme Ordeal.	Girl runs back upstairs as fast as she can with the ice cream and spoon, hearing the monster laughing at her, which is really scary.
Resurrection	Hero has second life-or-death moment, to see if learned lesson.	Girl feels the monster grab her leg, and monster turns out to be her mum, also hungry for ice cream.
Return with the Elixir	Hero returns home with treasure.	Girl and mum go back to her room and eat the whole tub.

PARENTAL RESPONSIBILITY AGREEMENT

SECTION 4(1)(B) THE CHILDREN ACT 1989

This agreement gives unmarried fathers equal parental responsibility under the law, including input in such important decisions such as where a child lives, his or her education, religion and medical treatment.

This is a parental responsibility agreement regarding:

Child's Name ·   Boy or Girl

....

Date of birth..

Date of 18th birthday...............................

Between the mother

Name..

Address..

....

and the father

Name..

Address..

....

We declare that we are the mother and father of the above child and we agree that the child's father shall have parental responsibility for the child (in addition to the mother having parental responsibility).

Signed *(Mother)*   Signed *(Father)*

....

Date......................................   Date..

The following evidence of identity was produced by the person signing above:

....

....

Signed in the presence of

Name of witness   Name of witness

....

Address...............................   Address...............................

....

Signature of witness   Signature of witness

....

[Justice of the Peace]   *[Justice of the Peace]*
[Justices' Clerk]   *[Justices' Clerk]*
[An Officer of the Court   *[An Officer of the Court*
authorised by a judge   *authorised by a judge*
to administer oaths]   *to administer oaths]*

....

FAMOUS ADOPTIVE PARENTS

Al Roker

Angelina Jolie

Barbara Walters

Bette Davis

Bob Hope

Burt Reynolds and
    Loni Anderson

Calista Flockhart

Cecil B. DeMille

Connie Chung and
    Maury Povich

Dan Marino

Diane Keaton

George Burns

George Lucas

Harry Belafonte

Henry Fonda

Isabella Rossellini

Jamie Lee Curtis

Jane Fonda

Jann Wenner

Jim Palmer

Joan Didion and
    John Gregory Dunne

John Denver

John McCain

Julie Andrews

Kirstie Alley

Kris Kristofferson

Kurt Vonnegut

Linda Ronstadt

Magic Johnson

Mia Farrow

Michelle Pfeiffer

Nicole Kidman and
    Tom Cruise

Oscar de la Renta

Ozzy Osbourne

Patti LaBelle

Paul Newman

Paul Simon

Ronald and Nancy Reagan

Rosie O'Donnell

Roy Rogers

Sammy Davis, Jr

Sharon Stone

Steven Spielberg and
    Kate Capshaw

Ted Danson

Walt Disney

Willie Mays

FAMOUS ADOPTED PEOPLE

Alexander the Great
Aristotle
Bill Clinton
Bo Diddley
Charles Dickens
Dave Thomas
Debbi Harry
Edgar Allen Poe
Edward Albee
Eleanor Roosevelt
George Washington Carver
Gerald Ford
Greg Louganis
Halle Berry
Ingrid Bergman
James Michener
Jean-Jacques Rousseau
Jesse Jackson
Jim Palmer
John J. Audubon

John Lennon
Langston Hughes
Leo Tolstoy
Louisa May Alcott
Malcolm X
Marilyn Monroe
Mark Twain
Melissa Gilbert
Mona Simpson
Moses
Nancy Reagan
Nat King Cole
Nelson Mandela
Priscilla Presley
Robert Byrd
Richard Burton
Sarah McLachlan
Scott Hamilton
Steve Jobs

THE HUMAN FAMILY TREE

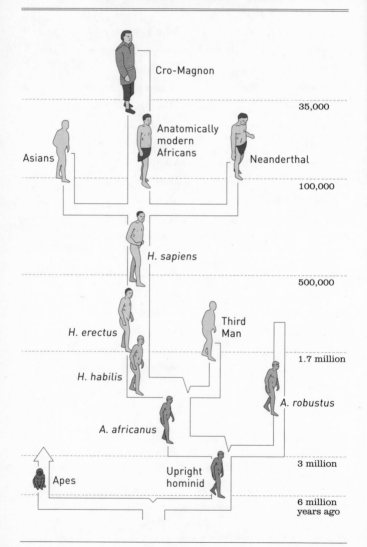

Cro-Magnon

35,000

Asians

Anatomically
modern
Africans

Neanderthal

100,000

H. sapiens

500,000

H. erectus

Third
Man

1.7 million

H. habilis

A. robustus

A. africanus

Apes

Upright
hominid

3 million

6 million
years ago

THE MALE EXPERIENCE
OF PREGNANCY:
SYMPTOMS OF THE COUVADE

cou • vade \kü-'väd\ *n* [F, fr. MF, cowardly inactivity, fr. *cover* to sit on, brood over]: the male experience of pregnancy and the male rituals performed around the time of childbirth

dressing in wife's clothing

mimicking childbirth

rushing to complete jobs
 around the home

abstention from intercourse

rearrangement of holidays

backache

depression

marital tension

extramarital affairs

drinking

restlessness

moving home

seclusion, either alone or
 with partner

moaning

mental illness

indigestion

colic

gastritis

food cravings

nausea and vomiting

increased or decreased
 appetite

weight gain

diarrhoea

constipation

headache

toothache

nosebleed

itch

muscle tremors

rashes

sties or cysts

anorexia

abdominal pain

bloating

HORMONAL CHANGES
DURING PREGNANCY

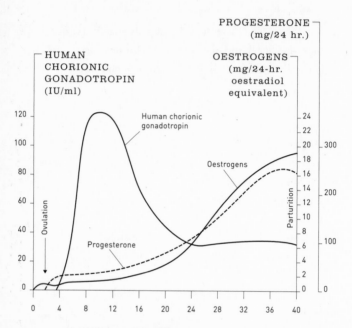

DURATION OF PREGNANCY (weeks)

abruptio placentae: premature separation of the placenta from the uterus

amniotomy: artificial rupture of membranes

andrologist: a doctor who specialises in the study of male reproduction

axoospermia: the absence of sperm in the seminal fluid

bloody show: vaginal bleeding late in pregnancy that often precedes labour

cephalopelvic disproportion: when the head of the foetus is too large to fit through the mother's pelvis

chadwick's sign: dark blue or purple discoloration of the vagina and cervix during pregnancy

chorion: outermost foetal membrane found around the amnion

cordocentesis: a test that obtains a blood sample from the umbilical cord while the foetus is still in utero

couvade syndrome: a phenomenon in which men show the symptoms of pregnancy

epididymis: the elongated organ in the male lying above and behind the testicles; contains a highly convoluted canal 4 to 6 metres in length where, after production, sperm are stored, nourished and ripened for a period of several months

fetoscopy: looking at the foetus in utero with a fibre-optic device

fimbria: the fingerlike projections at the end of the fallopian tubes

linea nigra: a darkened line that appears on the abdomen during pregnancy

lochia: the discharge present after delivery

mittelschmerz: the discomfort some women feel at the time ovulation occurs

occiput: back part of the head

parity: the fact of having borne a given number of children

polyhydramnios: excessive amount of amniotic fluid

sperm wash: technique for separating sperm from seminal fluid

vernix: the waxy, protective coating covering the skin of the foetus

GREEK GODS: THE FAMILY TREE

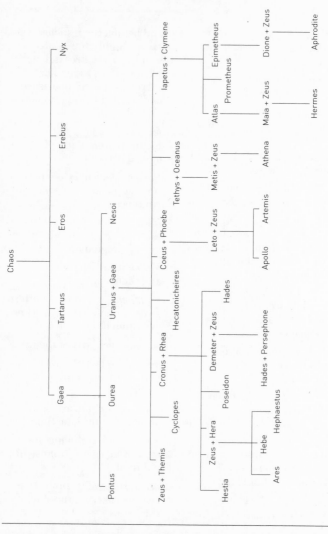

ESSENTIAL OILS AND FLOWER ESSENCES THAT MAY BE USEFUL WHEN TRYING TO CONCEIVE

Aspen For anticipation and anxiety, knowing that something (i.e. pregnancy) is about to happen, but not when and not fully understanding why you feel apprehensive.

Basil Reviving. May help tone the reproductive system.

Chamomile Calming and relaxing. Helps with gynaecological problems, including menstrual cramps. Combine with lavender or rose for massage.

Geranium A calming oil which is said to help balance the hormones. Combines well with rose.

Melissa (aka Lemon Balm) Uplifting. Also used for menstrual problems. Combines well with chamomile and rose.

Rose Powerful, restorative fragrance, with balancing effect on the mood. May help regulate the reproductive system.

Sandalwood Calming. Reputed to be an aphrodisiac, particularly for men.

She oak (Casuarina) Helps soothe emotional stress (such as caused by fertility issues) and overcomes female imbalances.

Vervain Calming. Useful for those who find it difficult to switch off and relax.

White Chestnut Anti-anxiety. Use in second half of menstrual cycle when you're wondering if the egg has been fertilised.

Willow Soothing. May ease resentment if one has not yet conceived, and thus help one do so.

Wisteria Promotes warm, sensual feelings in the body

NUMBER OF CHILDREN
ACCORDING TO YOUR PALM

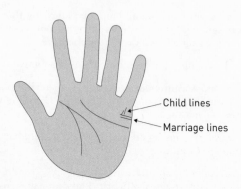

Child lines

Marriage lines

Horizontal lines located just below the base
of the little finger indicate marriages. Lines
that meet but do not cross a marriage line
indicate children that will be born into the
marriage.

NON-PHARMACEUTICAL WAYS
TO INDUCE LABOUR

Acupressure
(four fingers above the
inner ankle on the shin bone)

Black & blue cohosh

Castor oil

Cumin seed tea

Enema

Nipple stimulation

Pineapple

Sex

Spicy food

ANATOMY OF A DISPOSABLE NAPPY

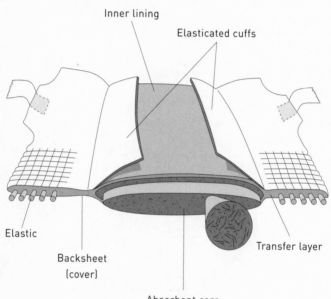

Inner lining

Elasticated cuffs

Elastic

Backsheet
(cover)

Transfer layer

Absorbent core
(cellulose and superabsorbent)

Liner: Carries urine, or 'the insult', quickly away from infant's skin. Feels soft to the touch. Typically made of polypropylene fibres spun into microscopic funnels that channel the insult towards the transfer layer.

Transfer Layer: Temporarily holds the insult en route to the core. Designed to move the insult laterally along the total surface of the nappy, preventing it from pooling where it first hit. Must provide sufficient volume to capture the insult, and must generate capillary force gradient towards the core to ensure rapid transfer, leaving the pore structure empty for the next insult.

Absorbent Core: Holds the insult, locking the liquid in gel form. Made of superabsorbent polymer flakes embedded in cellulose. The flakes can capture 300 times their weight in fluid and swell substantially in the present of an insult. Pulp disperses flakes to prevent a malfunction known as 'gel lock'.

Backsheet: Holds nappy together. Often made of a breathable film and a cloth-like backsheet. Materials are porous to reduce humidity in the nappy and to allow air to flow through to infant's skin.

Elasticated Cuff: Made of same material as liner, with elastic embedded. Prevents leaking down the leg and provides a snug fit.

WORD FOR 'MOTHER'
IN VARIOUS LANGUAGES

Afrikaans	*moeder*	Esperanto	*patrino*
Albanian	*mëmë*	Estonian	*ema*
	nënë	Eurish	*ameru*
Amharic	*innate*		*amelu*
Arabic	*om*	Farsi	*ma'dar*
Armenian	*mayr*	Finnish	*äiti*
Asturian	*ma*	French	*mère*
Azerbaijani	*ana*		*maman*
Basque	*ama*	Frisian	*mem*
Bengali	*ma*	Galician	*nai*
	amma		*mai*
Bosnian	*majka*	Georgian	*deda*
Breton	*ar vamm*	German	*mutter*
Bulgarian	*maika*	Greek	*mite'ra*
Cantonese	*ma-ma*	Gujarati	*maa*
Catalan	*mare*		*maataa*
Chipewyan	*eh-nehn*	Hawaiian	*makuahine*
Cornish	*mamm*	Hebrew	*ima*
	(an vamm)	Hindi	*mataji*
Creole	*manman*	Holooe	*ma-ma*
Croatian	*majka*	Hungarian	*anya*
Czech	*matka*	Icelandic	*mó£ir*
Dagaare	*ma*	Ido	*matro*
Danish	*mor*	Indonesian	*Ibu*
Dutch	*moeder*	Interlingua	*matre*
English	*mother*	Irish	*máthair*

Italian	*madre*	Slovak	*matka*
Japanese	*haha*	Slovenian	*mama*
	okaasan	Spanish	*madre*
Korean	*o-mo-ni*	Swahili	*mama*
Latin	*mater*	Swedish	*mamma*
Latvian	*ma-te*		*mor*
Lithuanian	*motina*	Tagalog	*nanay*
Luganda	*maama wange*		*ina*
Malaysian	*ibu*	Thai	*mae*
	emak	Tswana	*mme*
Mandarin	*ma-ma*		*mma*
Marshallese	*jinno*		*mama*
Mazahua	*ninána*	Turkish	*anne*
Norwegian	*mor*	Ukrainian	*maty*
Occitan	*maire*		*mama*
Polish	*matka*	Vietnamese	*me*
Portuguese	*mãe*		*má*
Quechua	*mama*	Welsh	*mam*
Romanian	*mamã*	Wolof	*yai*
Russian	*mat*	Xhosa	*mama*
Serbian	*majka*	Yiddish	*muter*
Sesotho	*mme*	Zulu	*umama*
Sinhala	*amma*		
	mava (formal)		

HOW LABOUR PROGRESSES:
THREE STUDIES

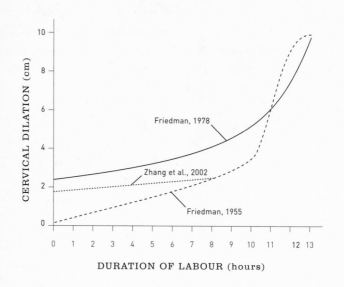

APGAR DECIPHERED

SIGN	0 POINTS	1 POINT	2 POINTS
A: ACTIVITY	Absent	Arms and legs flexed	Active movement
P: PULSE	Absent	Below 100 bpm	Above 100 bpm
G: GRIMACE	No response	Grimace	Sneezes, coughs, pulls away
A: APPEARANCE	Blue-grey, pale all over	Normal, except for extremities	Normal, over entire body
R: RESPIRATION	Absent	Slow, irregular	Good, crying

APGAR scores are given at one minute and five minutes after the birth. Scores of 7 to 10 are considered normal; 4 to 7 might require intervention; 3 and below demand immediate resuscitation.

BIRTHING POSITIONS

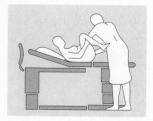

Lithotomy
On back, feet in stirrups. Risk of supine hypotension, increased risk of tearing or episiotomy.

Semi-sitting
During contractions, wrap hands around knees and pull knees up towards shoulders (as in squatting).

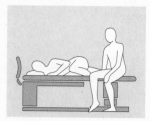

Lateral/Side-lying
Back curved, upper leg supported by partner. Gravity neutral, good for fast second stage.

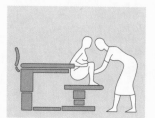

Squatting
Opens pelvis, gravity enhancing. Average pelvic outlet is 28% greater than in supine position.

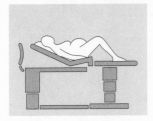

Trendelenburg's
Semi-recumbent with knees bent. Good for surgical interventions or manual expression.

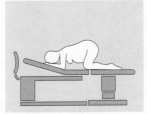

Hands and knees
Arch back for increased comfort. Uses gravity. Great for back labour, haemorrhoids.

Knee-Elbow
In multiparas with previous epidural. Good for particularly large children.

Dangle
Gravity, no external pressure on perineum/pelvis. Feeling of being well supported.

THE FIRST PRAM PATENT

PATENT #GB2668/1853

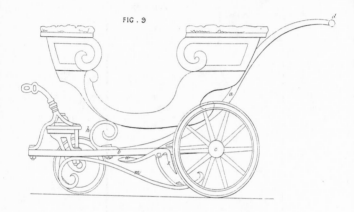

FIG . 9

The perambulator, or pram, was invented by English architect William Kent in 1733 for the 3rd Duke of Devonshire's children. The first pram patent was filed by Charles Burton on November 1853 and included improvements that allowed the carriage to be pushed from behind and taken apart for packing.

BASIC MONTESSORI PRINCIPLES

Children have absorbent minds.

Children desire independence.

Children have sensitive times.

Children develop in stages.

Children are eager to learn.

Children should be taught
through all their senses.

Children should be given
the opportunity to develop
their full potential.

Children should be allowed
to learn independently.

Children should be given freedom
and choices within a structured
environment.

BIRTHMARKS

Angel kisses: Pinkish, irregularly shaped patches on the face. Usually disappear over time. If on the nape of the neck, known as stork bites.

Café au lait marks: Permanent patches that are darker than surrounding skin. Tan or light brown on light-skinned children, dark brown on dark-skinned children. May be present at birth or appear during childhood. If baby born with six or more, consult doctor.

Cavernous haemangioma: Reddish or bluish-red with lumpy texture. Grow in size during first year, and then decrease. Typically half gone by age 5 and fully gone by age 12.

Congenital pigmented naevi: Shades ranging from tan to black; some have hair. Only cause for concern if they are very large, bleed, or change color, shape, or size. Also known as the common mole.

Mongolian spots: Temporary accumulations of pigment under the skin, typically on the bottom or back. Blue or grey, like a bruise. Most common in babies of African, Asian or East Indian descent. Fade during first few years.

Port wine stains: Large, flat, irregularly shaped red or purple areas caused by excess blood vessels under the skin. Can be removed by plastic surgeon or dermatologist. Do not disappear over time.

Skin tags: Small, soft, flesh-coloured or pigmented growths of skin. Can be removed.

Spider naevi: Thin, dilated blood vessels with spiderlike shape. Often fade during first year.

Stork bites: Pinkish, irregularly shaped patches at the nape of the neck. Usually disappear over time. If on the face, known as angel kisses.

Strawberry haemangioma: White or pale, turning red over time. Raised, soft texture, caused by irregular blood supply. Range in size from pea to larger than a cricket ball. Most disappear on own between age 5 and age 9 years. May be removed surgically.

WAVEFORM OF A BABY'S CRY

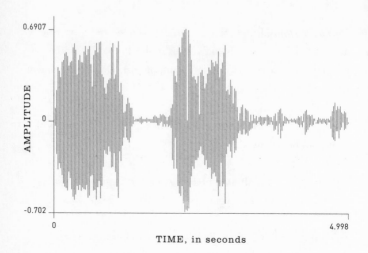

WONG/BAKER FACES PAIN SCALE

0	1	2	3	4	5
No Hurt	Hurts Little Bit	Hurts Little More	Hurts Even More	Hurts Whole Lot	Hurts Worst

CLASSIC LULLABY LYRICS

Brahms's Lullaby
Lullaby and good night, with roses bedight
With lilies o'er spread is baby's wee bed
Lay thee down now and rest, may thy slumber be blessed
Lay thee down now and rest, may thy slumber be blessed
Lullaby and good night, thy mother's delight
Bright angels beside my darling abide
They will guard thee at rest, thou shalt wake on my breast
They will guard thee at rest, thou shalt wake on my breast.

Frère Jacques (Are You Sleeping?)
Frère Jacques, Frère Jacques,
Dormez-vous? Dormez-vous?
Sonnez les matines, sonnez les matines
Ding ding dong, ding ding dong.

(English Version)
Are you sleeping, are you sleeping?
Brother John, Brother John?
Morning bells are ringing, morning bells are ringing
Ding ding dong, ding ding dong.

Sleep Baby Sleep

Sleep, baby, sleep
Your father tends the sheep
Your mother shakes the dreamland tree
And from it fall sweet dreams for thee
Sleep, baby, sleep
Sleep, baby, sleep.

Sleep, baby, sleep
Our cottage vale is deep
The little lamb is on the green
With snowy fleece so soft and clean
Sleep, baby, sleep
Sleep, baby, sleep.

Twinkle, Twinkle, Little Star

Twinkle, twinkle, little star
How I wonder what you are!
Up above the world so high
Like a diamond in the sky
Twinkle, twinkle, little star
How I wonder what you are.

Hush, Little Baby
Hush, little baby, don't say a word
Papa's gonna buy you a mockingbird
And if that mockingbird won't sing,
Papa's gonna buy you a diamond ring
And if that diamond ring turns brass,
Papa's gonna buy you a looking glass
And if that looking glass gets broke,
Papa's gonna buy you a billy goat
And if that billy goat won't pull,
Papa's gonna buy you a cart and bull
And if that cart and bull fall down,
You'll still be the sweetest little baby in town.

All the Pretty Horses
Hush-a-bye, don't you cry,
Go to sleep-y, little baby
When you wake you shall have
All the pretty little horses
Blacks and bays, dapple greys,
Coach and six white horses
Hush-a-bye, don't you cry,
Go to sleep-y, little baby.

Golden Slumbers

Golden slumbers kiss your eyes,

Smiles await you when you rise.

Sleep, pretty baby,

Do not cry,

And I'll sing you a lullaby

Care you know not,

Therefore sleep,

While I o'er you watch do keep.

Sleep, pretty darling,

Do not cry,

And I will sing a lullaby.

DIAGRAM OF A SKINNER BOX

A Skinner box is a behaviour-modification tool that contains at least one manipulandum (such as a response lever or key), at least one primary reinforcer (such as food, water or shock), and at least one stimulus (such as a light or bell). In the diagram, each time the pigeon hears a command through the speaker and pecks at the key, he gains access to grain. American psychologist B. F. Skinner (1904–1990) built such a box for his infant daughter. Though not a commercial success, it was effective in the lab.

FIRST WORDS FOR
A BOWEL MOVEMENT

Aa Aa (German)

caca

do-do

dobby

dong (Korean)

doo

doodie

doo-doo

dookie

dookie doo

jobby (Glaswegian)

kaka

kakashka (Russian)

keech (Glasgow)

kuso (Japanese)

pichin (Spanish & Italian)

plonk (Norwegian)

poop

poopie

poopies

poopoo

poo-poo

poopsey

poopsters

stinky

tahi (Malay)

turd

tutti (Hindi)

uchra (Arabic)

unko (Japanese)

yukky

CAROL BURNETT
ON CHILDBIRTH

U.S. COMEDIAN, 1936–

'If you want to know the feeling [of labour pain], just take your bottom lip and pull it over your head.'

SCIENTIFIC TERMS
TO DESCRIBE CRYING

cry: The total sound response to a specific stimulus. This may contain many cry units.

cry type or mode: One of four acoustic outputs an infant may exhibit during a cry unit. (See *phonation, hyperphonation, dysphonation* and *inspiratory phonation.*)

cry unit: The sound that results during the passage of air past the vocal cords during a single inspiratory/expiratory cycle.

frequency spectrum: The frequency content of a signal.

fundamental frequency: A physical characteristic of all periodic waveforms. Measured in cycles per second or hertz (Hz), it refers to the number of times a complex waveform repeats itself in one second.

harmonic: A multiple of the fundamental frequency. For example, if the fundamental frequency is 100 Hz, the first harmonic is 200 Hz, the second is 300 Hz, and so on.

hyperphonation: A segment of a cry unit that is periodic and typically has a fundamental frequency from 1,000 Hz to 2,000 Hz.

inspiratory phonation: Any sound produced during inspiration.

inspiration: The act of drawing air into the lungs.

octave: A bandwidth in which the highest frequency is double the lowest frequency. For example, 100–200 Hz or 800–1,600 Hz.

phonation: A segment of a cry unit that is periodic and typically has a fundamental frequency from 250 Hz to 700 Hz.

NAPPY FOLDING METHODS

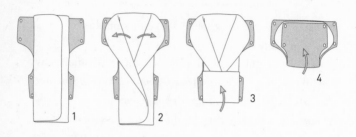

BASIC PINLESS PREFOLD

1. Fold thin sides of prefold over the thick centre and place in wrap.
2. Fan out back.
3. Place baby in nappy, fold up front.
4. Close wrap.

THE PREFOLD TWIST

1. Lay prefold flat and open.
2. Bring left front corner over and to right and right front corner under and to left.
3. Place baby in nappy and bring front up between legs and pin sides.

BASIC PINNED PREFOLD

1. Fold front sides to centre and fold back down.
2. Fold edge of front up.
3. Place baby in nappy, fold up front.
4. Pin sides.

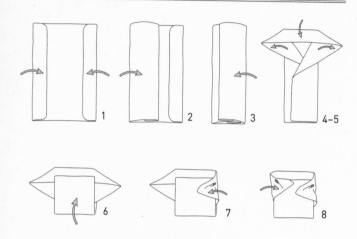

FLAT 2–5–2 PREFOLD

1. Lay flat nappy open and fold both sides towards centre about 8 to 10 centimetres.
2. Fold left side in so that an 8- to 10-centimetre strip is in centre of nappy.
3. Fold right side in so that an 8- to 10-centimetre strip is in centre of nappy. (You should now have five layers in the centre of the nappy and two layers on either side.)
4. Fan out back of nappy.
5. Fold back of nappy down.
6. Fold front of nappy towards centre. Place baby in nappy and then bring front up between baby's legs.
7. Bring right back corner to front panel and pin.
8. Bring left back corner to front panel and pin.

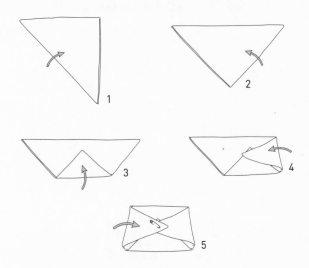

FLAT NAPPY TRIANGLE FOLD

1. Fold nappy into a triangle by bringing diagonal corners together.
2. Fold triangle in half along longest side to make a smaller triangle that is four layers thick.
3. Place baby in nappy and bring up front.
4. Bring corners together to meet in centre of baby's tummy.
5. Pin in centre.

FIRST-YEAR MILESTONES:
A HUMAN INFANT VS
A CAPTIVE-BORN CHIMPANZEE

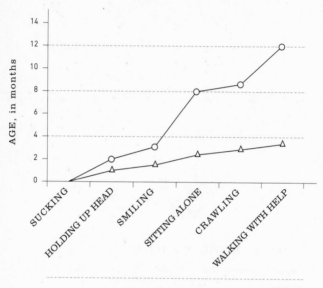

O Human infant

△ Infant captive born chimpanzee

CAFFEINE-INDUCED ORGANIC
MENTAL DISORDER

CAFFEINE-INDUCED ORGANIC MENTAL DISORDER
305.90 CAFFEINE INTOXICATION
(From *Desk Reference to the Diagnostic Criteria from DSM-3-R:*
American Psychiatric Association, 1987)

A. Recent consumption of caffeine, usually in excess of 250 mg.

B. At least five of the following signs:
    1. restlessness
    2. nervousness
    3. excitement
    4. insomnia
    5. flushed face
    6. diuresis
    7. gastrointestinal disturbance
    8. muscle twitching
    9. rambling flow of thought and speech
    10. tachycardia or cardiac arrhythmia
    11. periods of inexhaustibility
    12. psychomotor agitation

COPING MECHANISMS:
THE FOUR NOBLE TRUTHS,
ACCORDING TO BUDDHA

THE FIRST NOBLE TRUTH: THE EXISTENCE OF SUFFERING

'Now this, monks, is the noble truth of pain (dukkha): birth is painful, old age is painful, sickness is painful, death is painful, sorrow, lamentation, dejection and despair are painful. Contact with unpleasant things is painful, not getting what one wishes is painful. In short, the five components of existence are painful.'

THE SECOND NOBLE TRUTH: THE CAUSE OF SUFFERING

'Now this, monks, is the noble truth of the cause of pain: the craving, which tends to rebirth, combined with pleasure and lust, finding pleasure here and there; namely, the craving for passion, the craving for existence, the craving for nonexistence.'

THE THIRD NOBLE TRUTH: THE END OF SUFFERING

'Now this, monks, is the noble truth of the path that leads to the cessation of pain: the cessation without a remainder of craving, the abandonment, forsaking, release, nonattachment.'

THE FOURTH NOBLE TRUTH: THE END OF PAIN BY WAY OF THE EIGHTFOLD PATH

'Now this, monks, is the noble truth of the path that leads to the cessation of pain: this is the noble Eightfold Path.'

NIRVANA

'Right Concentration, Right Mindfulness, Right Effort, Right Livelihood, Right Action, Right Speech, Right Resolve, Right View.'

METHODS OF STERILISATION

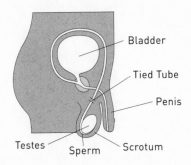

VASECTOMY
The vas deferens, the tubes that deliver the sperm from the testes to mix with the seminal fluids, is cut and tied, or closed.

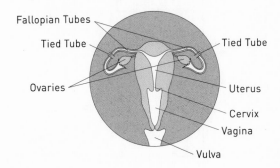

TUBAL LIGATION
The fallopian tubes, the tubes that deliver the egg from the ovary to the uterus, are cut and tied, or closed.

SOME MILESTONES IN THE FIRST 18 MONTHS

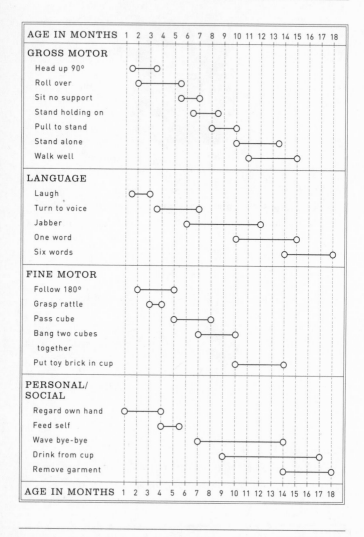

AGE IN MONTHS	1	2	3	4	5	6	7	8	9	10	11	12	13	14	15	16	17	18

GROSS MOTOR
- Head up 90°: 2–3
- Roll over: 2–5
- Sit no support: 5–6
- Stand holding on: 6–7½
- Pull to stand: 7½–9
- Stand alone: 10–14
- Walk well: 11–18

LANGUAGE
- Laugh: 2–3
- Turn to voice: 4–7
- Jabber: 5½–11
- One word: 10–15
- Six words: 14–18

FINE MOTOR
- Follow 180°: 3–5
- Grasp rattle: 3–4
- Pass cube: 5–7
- Bang two cubes together: 7–9
- Put toy brick in cup: 10–14

PERSONAL/ SOCIAL
- Regard own hand: 2–4
- Feed self: 4–5
- Wave bye-bye: 7–13
- Drink from cup: 9–17
- Remove garment: 14–18

AGE IN MONTHS	1	2	3	4	5	6	7	8	9	10	11	12	13	14	15	16	17	18

DR ARNOLD GESELL ON INFANCY

U.S. CHILD PSYCHOLOGIST, 1880–1961

'It is man's distinction that he has the longest infancy. . . . Some creatures have virtually no infancy at all. Some birds are so precocious that they fly immediately on hatching. The golden eaglet, however, requires 11 weeks before it spreads its giant wings in full flight. Not until the age of 12 weeks is it buffeted by its parents and driven forcibly from the home by them. The guinea pig shifts for himself 3 days after birth. It takes the white rat as many weeks. The chimpanzee becomes an adult at the age of 9 years. The more complex and advanced the mature organism, the longer the period of infancy.'

HOW TO ANALYSE YOUR INFANT'S SKULL: BASIC PHRENOLOGY

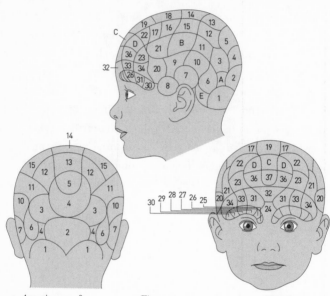

1. Amativeness & Conjugal Love
2. Parental Love
3. Friendship
4. Inhabitiveness
5. Continuity
6. Combativeness
7. Destructiveness
8. Alimentiveness
9. Aquisitiveness
10. Secretiveness
11. Cautiousness
12. Approbativeness
13. Self-Esteem
14. Firmness
15. Conscientiousness
16. Hope
17. Spirituality
18. Benevolence
19. Constructiveness
20. Ideality
21. Sublimity
22. Initiation
23. Mirth
24. Individuality
25. Form
26. Size
27. Weight
28. Colour
29. Order
30. Calculation
31. Locality
32. Eventuality
33. Time
34. Tune
35. Language
36. Causality
37. Comparison
C. Human Nature
D. Suavity

BASIC DEVELOPMENTAL PSYCHOLOGY

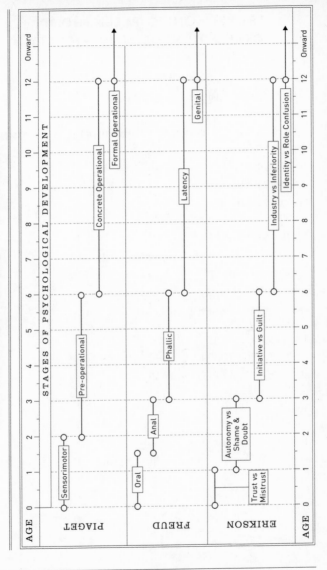

STAGES OF PSYCHOLOGICAL DEVELOPMENT

TRANSITION TO PARENTHOOD:
TOTAL ADJUSTMENT DIFFICULTY

Researchers have quantified the various factors contributing
to the difficult transition to parenthood.

ITEM	OVERALL	FATHERS	MOTHERS
Baby's crying	.52	.61	.42
Missing sleep	.49	.47	.50
Not enough time for job	.21	.20	.28
Not enough time for family	.05	.30	.04
Less time with spouse	.48	.61	.39
Being tied down to home	.19	.28	.05
Change long-range plans	.39	.50	.05
Additional expenses	.49	.60	.26
Need more knowledge about parenting	.20	.06	.47
Less income, spouse not working	.17	.20	.24
Changing nappies	.30	.20	.51
Feeding the baby	.51	.46	.58
Visits from friends and relatives	.34	.18	.46
More cooking and housework	.44	.49	.38

24-HOUR NEWBORN DAY

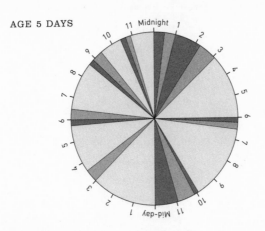

AGE 5 DAYS

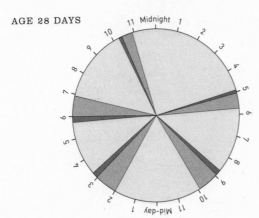

AGE 28 DAYS

SLEEPING   FEEDING   CRYING

CLINICAL SYMPTOMS OF
SLEEP DEPRIVATION

Tiredness

Irritability

Memory loss

Frequent infections

Blurred vision

Itching eyes

Burning eyes

Appetite loss

Food cravings

Constipation

Diarrhoea

Excessive wind

Nodding off during sedentary activities
(microsleeps)

Depression

Vocabulary loss

Disorientation

Hallucination

Psychosis

Chills

Apathy

Anxiety

Dread

Loss of control

PROFILES OF THE BREAST:
PRE- AND POST-LACTATION

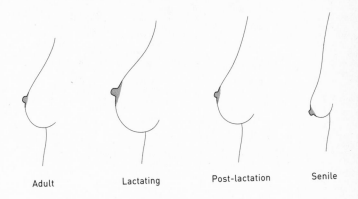

Adult   Lactating   Post-lactation   Senile

DAYS TO DOUBLE BIRTH WEIGHT
FOR VARIOUS SPECIES

Human	180
Horse	60
Cow	47
Reindeer	30
Goat	19
Sheep	19
Dog	8
Cat	7
Rat	4–5

SEAT BELT LAWS FOR CARS, TAXIS AND PRIVATE CARS, BY AGE AND HEIGHT

	FRONT SEAT	REAR SEAT	WHOSE RESPONSIBILITY?
Child under 3 years old	Appropriate child restraint must be worn.	Appropriate child restraint must be worn if available.	Driver
Child aged 3 to 11 and under 1.5 metres in height	Appropriate child restraint must be worn if available. If not, adult seat belt must be worn.	Appropriate child restraint must be worn if available. If not, adult seat belt must be worn.	Driver
Child aged 12 or 13 or younger child 1.5 metres or more in height	Adult seat belt must be worn if available.	Adult seat belt must be worn if available.	Driver
Passengers over the age of 14	Adult seat belt must be worn if available.	Adult seat belt must be worn if available.	Passenger

CHILD LABOUR LAWS

The youngest age a child can work is 13 years old, except if that child is involved in television, theatre, modelling or similar activities.

Children aged 10 or over may be employed on an occasional basis by and under the direct supervision of their parents in light agricultural work or horticultural work.

Children may not work:
- without an employment permit issued by the local education authority.
- in any industrial setting.
- during school hours.
- before 7a.m. or after 7p.m.
- for more than one hour before school.
- for more than four hours without taking a break of at least one hour.
- in any occupations prohibited by local by-laws or other legislation (e.g. pubs, betting shops).
- in any work that may be harmful to their health, well-being or education without having a two-week break from any work during the school holidays in each calendar year.

During term time children may work a maximum of 12 hours
per week, of which:
- a maximum of two hours on school days and Sundays.
- a maximum of five hours on Saturdays for 13- to 14-year olds, or eight hours for 15- to 16-year olds.

During school holidays 13- to 14-year olds may work a maximum
of 25 hours per week, of which:
- a maximum of five hours on weekdays and Saturdays.
- a maximum of two hours on Sundays.

During school holidays 15- to 16-year olds may work a maximum of 35 hours per week, of which:
- a maximum of eight hours on weekdays and Saturdays.
- a maximum of two hours on Sundays.

GETTING TO SLEEP

Mindell: Develop a calm, soothing and consistent bedtime routine. Put your baby to bed drowsy but awake, so he learns to soothe self to sleep.

Ferber: Take a close look at your bedtime routine. Put baby down when still awake so she learns to settle self to sleep, both when you first put her down and if she wakes up during the night.

The AAP: Create routine and give baby transitional object, such as blanket or stuffed animal. Put baby down while sleepy but awake.

Brazelton: Don't put baby to sleep by rocking in your arms, nursing or bottle. Instead, get baby in bed while awake, then generally reassure without words.

Sears: Baby needs to be 'parented' to sleep. Rock, feed, pace as you hold baby, establishing and following a regular ritual.

CO-SLEEPING

Mindel: Do what's right for you. But note that children who share a bed with parents have a harder time learning to fall asleep on their own. Be sure the sleep environment is safe (e.g., no pillows or duvets).

Ferber: Bad idea. People sleep better alone. Okay if child is sick or very upset, but it's better to encourage baby to see self as independent individual with own bed.

The AAP: Avoid letting child sleep with you. Baby will never learn to sleep on his own.

Brazelton: Acceptable, but remember baby will eventually need to sleep independently. May be difficult to get baby in own bed. Be consistent night to night.

Sears: Best arrangement. Easy for breastfeeding. Mother and baby sleep better knowing each other is secure.

BABY WON'T STAY ASLEEP

Mindell: Help baby back to sleep. If waking continues for a few weeks, resort to checking routine. Stay in baby's room for brief time, keeping contact neutral, and don't pick up. Leave and return in five-minute intervals, gradually increasing time you are gone.

Ferber: If baby is at least five months old, try letting him cry for progressively longer intervals of time, starting at five minutes, increasing to ten, and so on. Between intervals, spend two to three minutes with baby, talking and patting. Don't pick him up or rock.

The AAP: If baby isn't sleeping eight hours at a stretch, keep awake longer and play in the afternoon and early evening. Also increase the amount of his before-bed feeding.

Brazelton: If baby wakes up after only a few hours, let her find her own way back to sleep using self-comforting techniques such as thumbsucking. When she wakes, don't feed, jump up, or go to baby at first cry.

Sears: Try to find source of his wakefulness (dirty nappy, hunger, upset routines during the day, etc.). Increase daytime attachment to you, and have parents take turns helping baby back to sleep.

THE PRIMARY TEETH

Refer to chart as if you are looking into a child's mouth.

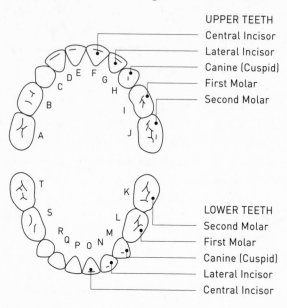

UPPER TEETH
Central Incisor
Lateral Incisor
Canine (Cuspid)
First Molar
Second Molar

LOWER TEETH
Second Molar
First Molar
Canine (Cuspid)
Lateral Incisor
Central Incisor

UPPER TEETH	ERUPT	SHED
Central Incisor	8–12 months	6–7 years
Lateral Incisor	9–13 months	7–8 years
Canine (Cuspid)	16–22 months	10–12 years
First Molar	13–19 months	9–11 years
Second Molar	25–33 months	10–12 years

LOWER TEETH	ERUPT	SHED
Second Molar	23–31 months	10–12 years
First Molar	14–18 months	9–11 years
Canine (Cuspid)	17–23 months	9–12 years
Lateral Incisor	10–16 months	7–8 years
Central Incisor	6–10 months	6–7 years

THE EFFECTS OF A BOY CHILD
ON MARRIAGE AND MONEY

Marriages with sons are more stable than those with daughters.

Fathers are more involved with the family if they have sons than if they have daughters.

Parents in families with sons tend to play more traditional roles than parents in families with only daughters.

Couples whose first child is a son tend to have subsequent children sooner.

Men work about 40 hours a year more after the birth of a son relative to a daughter.

Hourly earnings of fathers of sons increase more after childbirth than do the earnings of fathers of daughters.

Families with a son spend 4 to 7 percent more on housing compared to families with a daughter.

There are no significant effects of child gender on purchases of durables, such as cars or furniture.

Families with a girl spend more money on clothing than families with a boy.

Families with a boy spend nearly 10 percent more on beauty salons and health clubs than families with a girl.

The average difference in spending between one-son and one-daughter families is £3,000 per year.

(Taken from *Investment in Sons and Daughters* by Shelly Lundberg and Elaina Rose, University of Washington, 2002.)

SOME CHILD STARS AND THE AGE AT WHICH THEY PLAYED THEIR FIRST MAJOR ROLE

STAR	AGE	TV/FILM ROLE
Drew Barrymore	7	Gertie, *ET the Extra Terrestrial*, 1982
Danny Bonaduce	10	Danny Partridge, *The Partridge Family*, 1970–74
Lauren Chapin	9	Kathy 'Kitten' Anderson, *Father Knows Best*, 1954–60
Todd Bridges	13	Willis Jackson, *Diff'rent Strokes*, 1978–86
Gary Coleman	10	Arnold Jackson, *Diff'rent Strokes*, 1978–86
Brandon Cruz	7	Eddie Corbett, *The Courtship of Eddie's Father*, 1969–72
Macaulay Culkin	10	Kevin McCallister, *Home Alone*, 1990
Claire Danes	15	Angela Chase, *My So-Called Life*, 1994–95
Jodie Foster	12	Audrey, *Alice Doesn't Live Here Anymore*, 1974
Annette Funicello	13	*The Mickey Mouse Club*, 1955–59
Melissa Gilbert	10	Laura Ingalls, *Little House on the Prairie*, 1974–82
Billy Gray	16	Bud Anderson, *Father Knows Best*, 1954–60
Rupert Grint	13	Ron Weasley, *Harry Potter*, 2001
Ron Howard	6	Opie Taylor, *The Andy Griffith Show*, 1960–68
Helen Hunt	12	Helga Robinson, *Swiss Family Robinson*, 1975–76
Anissa Jones	8	Buffy Jones, *Family Affair*, 1966–71

Emmanuel Lewis	12	Webster Long, *Webster*, 1983–87
Stanley Livingston	10	Chip Douglas, *My Three Sons*, 1960–72
Hayley Mills	13	Gillie, *Tiger Bay*, 1959
Ricky Nelson	12	Ricky Nelson, *The Adventures of Ozzie & Harriet*, 1952–66
Jay North	7	Dennis Mitchell, *Dennis the Menace*, 1959–63
Mary-Kate & Ashley Olsen	6 mths.	Michele Tanner, *Full House*, 1987–95
Haley Joel Osment	11	Cole, *The Sixth Sense*, 1999
Anna Paquin	11	Flora, *The Piano*, 1993
Paul Peterson	13	Jeff Stone, *The Donna Reed Show*, 1958–66
Jon Provost	7	Timmy Martin, *Lassie*, 1957–64
Daniel Radcliffe	10	David, *David Copperfield*, 1999
Tommy Rettig	13	Jeff Miller, *Lassie*, 1954–57
Adam Rich	9	Nicholas Bradford, *Eight Is Enough*, 1977–81
Fred Savage	11	Kevin Arnold, *The Wonder Years*, 1988–93
Ricky Schroeder	12	Ricky Stratton, *Silver Spoons*, 1982–87
Shirley Temple	7	*Bright Eyes*, 1935; *Poor Little Rich Girl*, 1936
Tiffany Amber-Thiessen	15	Kelly Kapowski, *Saved by the Bell*, 1989–94
Jonathan Taylor Thomas	10	Randy Taylor, *Home Improvement*, 1991–99
Johnny Whitaker	7	Jody Davis, *Family Affair*, 1966–77
Emma Watson	11	Hermione Granger, *Harry Potter*, 2001

TOP 99 WORDS: PERCENTAGE OF CHILDREN REPORTED UNDERSTANDING OR PRODUCING AT ONE YEAR

aeroplane	3.4	car	4.5
all gone	4.5	cat	9.1
apple	2.3	cheese	6.8
aunt	2.3	choo choo	4.5
baby	14.8	cookie	11.4
baby sitter's name	3.4	cow	2.3
bad	2.3	cracker	5.7
ball	22.7	cup	2.3
balloon	4.5	daddy	55.7
banana	8.0	dog	28.4
bath	6.8	doll	2.3
biscuit	11.4	door	2.3
bear	4.5	duck	13.6
bicycle	2.3	eat	2.3
big	2.3	eye	8.0
bird	13.6	fish	6.8
blow	2.3	flower	3.4
blue	2.3	food	2.3
book	5.7	foot	2.3
bottle	15.9	go	4.5
bread	3.4	grandma	8.0
brother	4.5	grandpa	6.8
bubbles	3.4	grr	17.0
bunny	2.3	hat	3.4
bye	47.7	hello	5.7

hi	42.0	puppy	2.3
horse	3.4	pussy	18.2
hot	5.7	quack	12.5
it	2.3	see	4.5
juice	8.0	shh	11.4
keys	3.4	shoe	10.2
light	4.5	sister	2.3
love	2.3	sky	2.3
me	2.3	sock	8.0
miaow	8.0	telephone	2.3
mummy	53.4	thank you	11.4
moo	5.7	that	3.4
moon	2.3	this	2.3
more	2.3	tickle	2.3
mouse	2.3	tree	5.7
mouth	2.3	uh oh	35.2
nice	2.3	vroom	14.8
night night	11.4	water	10.2
no	20.5	what	5.7
nose	5.7	where	2.3
ouch	12.5	woof	21.6
owie	6.8	yes	6.8
pat-a-cake	6.8	yucky	3.4
peekaboo	5.7	yum yum	22.7
pretty	4.5		

voice sounds: Produced by a flow of air from the lungs causing the vocal cords to vibrate ('u' as in *cup*). All vowels are voice sounds.

voiceless sounds: Produced by flow of air without vibration from the vocal cords ('p' as in *pit;* 'f' as in *fun*).

fricatives: Consonants produced by rapid changes in pressure constricted through air passage cavities. They come in voiced and unvoiced pairs ('z', 's').

plosives: Consonants produced by brief obstructing of vocal track so sound comes in quick bursts. They are also paired ('p', 'b').

nasals: Voiced consonants in which sound passes through the nose (*man*).

ACKNOWLEDGEMENTS

First of all, we are truly and deeply grateful to our husbands: Amy to Martin Gammon and Liz to Dan Duane. Without them, this would have never happened.

We are also both deeply indebted to our dear friend, Natasha Bondy.

Many others offered invaluable inspiration, suggestions, expertise, patience, research and support: Michael Benedek, Ivor Brown, Kris Dahl, Jared Diamond, Kelly Duane, Kit Duane, Karen Flood, Eric Freitag, Renate Gammon, Christine Glastonbury, Alison Gopnik, Max Jones, Sarah Jones, Allison Keene, David Kestenbaum, Anton Krukowski, Judy Laghi, Russ LaMotte, Shelly Lundberg, Sarah Malarkey, Ben Maniatis, Chris Maniatis, Elizabeth Maniatis, Kathleen Maniatis, Nick Maniatis, Patricia Maniatis, Ted Maniatis, Terez Maniatis, Theo Maniatis, Daphne Maurer, Emily Newman, Jay Schaefer, Colleen Shelly, Bill Taylor, Debbie Weil, Doug Weil, Judy Weil, and Jil Weinstock.

AUTHORS

AMY MANIATIS is a marketing executive. She is the mother of Lucy, 5, and Chloe, 3, and she lives in Berkeley, California.

ELIZABETH WEIL is a journalist whose writing appears in *The New York Times Magazine*, *Time*, and many other places. She is the mother of Hannah, 2, and lives in San Francisco, California.